1

Grammar Connection

STRUCTURE THROUGH CONTENT

D1502317

SERIES EDITORS

Marianne Celce-Murcia

M. E. Sokolik

Jill Korey O'Sullivan

NATIONAL
GEOGRAPHIC
LEARNING

CENGAGE
Learning·

Australia • Brazil • Japan • Korea • Mexico • Singapore • Spain • United Kingdom • United States

Grammar Connection 1: Structure Through Content
Jill Korey O'Sullivan

Senior Editors: Marianne Celce-Murcia,
   M.E. Sokolik

Publisher, Academic ESL: James W. Brown

Executive Editor, Dictionaries & Adult ESL:
   Sherrise Roehr

Director of Content Development:
   Anita Raducanu

Director of Product Marketing: Amy Mabley

Product Marketing Manager: Laura Needham

Senior Field Marketing Manager:
   Donna Lee Kennedy

Cover Image: Larry Brownstein/Photodisc Red/
   Getty/RF

Editor, Academic ESL: Tom Jefferies

Editorial Assistant: Katherine Reilly

Associate Production Editor: Erika Hokanson

Manufacturing Buyer: Betsy Donaghey

Production Project Manager: Chrystie Hopkins

Production Services:
   InContext Publishing Partners

Index: Alexandra Nickerson

Cover and Interior Designer: Linda Beaupre

Credits appear on page 244, which constitutes a
continuation of the copyright page.

For permission to use material from this text or product,
submit all requests online at **www.cengage.com/permissions**
Further permissions questions can be emailed to
permissionrequest@cengage.com

Library of Congress Control Number: 20066901327

ISBN-13: 978-1-4130-0830-2

ISBN-10: 1-4130-0830-5

National Geographic Learning
20 Channel Center Street
Boston, MA 02210
USA

Cengage Learning is a leading provider of customized learning solutions with office locations around the globe, including Singapore, the United Kingdom, Australia, Mexico, Brazil, and Japan.

Cengage Learning products are represented in Canada by Nelson Education, Ltd.

Visit National Geographic Learning online at **ngl.cengage.com**

Visit our corporate website at **www.cengage.com**

Printed in the United States of America
5 6 7 16 15 14 13

Contents

 Using language grammatically and being able to communicate authentically are important goals for students. My grammar research suggests that students' mastery of grammar improves when they interpret and produce grammar in meaningful contexts at the discourse level. *Grammar Connection* connects learners to academic success, allowing them to reach their goals and master the grammar.

— Marianne Celce-Murcia

 "Connections" is probably the most useful concept in any instructor's vocabulary. To help students connect what they are learning to the rest of their lives is the most important task I fulfill as an instructor. *Grammar Connection* lets instructors and students find those connections. The series connects grammar to reading, writing, and speaking. It also connects students with the ability to function academically, to use the Internet for interesting research, and to collaborate with others on projects and presentations. — M. E. Sokolik

Dear Instructor,

With experience in language teaching, teacher training, and research, we created *Grammar Connection* to be uniquely relevant for academically and professionally oriented courses and students. Every lesson in the series deals with academic content to help students become familiar with the language of college and the university and to feel more comfortable in all of their courses, not just English.

While academic content provides the context for this series, our goal is for the learner to go well beyond sentence-level exercises in order to use grammar as a resource for comprehending and producing academic discourse. Students move from shorter, more controlled exercises to longer, more self-directed, authentic ones. Taking a multi-skills approach, *Grammar Connection* includes essential grammar that students need to know at each level. Concise lessons allow instructors to use the material easily in any classroom situation.

We hope that you and your students find our approach to the teaching and learning of grammar for academic and professional purposes in *Grammar Connection* effective and innovative.

Marianne Celce-Murcia
Series Editor

M. E. Sokolik
Series Editor

Welcome to
Grammar Connection

■ What is *Grammar Connection*?

Grammar Connection is a five-level grammar series that integrates content with grammar instruction in an engaging format to prepare students for future academic and professional success.

■ What is the content?

The content in *Grammar Connection* is drawn from various academic disciplines: sociology, psychology, medical sciences, computer science, communications, biology, engineering, business, and the social sciences.

■ Why does *Grammar Connection* incorporate content into the lessons?

The content is used to provide high-interest contexts for exploring the grammar. The charts and exercises are contextualized with the content in each lesson. Learning content is not the focus of *Grammar Connection*—it sets the scene for learning grammar.

■ Is *Grammar Connection* "discourse-based"?

Yes. With *Grammar Connection*, learners go beyond sentence-level exercises in order to use grammar as a resource for comprehending and producing academic discourse. These discourses include conversations, narratives, and exposition.

■ Does *Grammar Connection* include communicative practice?

Yes. *Grammar Connection* takes a multi-skills approach. The series includes listening activities as well as texts for reading, and the production tasks elicit both spoken and written output via pair or group work tasks.

■ Why are the lessons shorter than in other books?

Concise lessons allow instructors to use the material easily in any classroom situation. For example, one part of a lesson could be covered in a 50-minute period, allowing instructors with shorter class times to feel a sense of completion. Alternatively, a single lesson could fit into a longer, multi-skills class period. For longer, grammar-focused classes, more than one lesson could be covered.

■ Does *Grammar Connection* include opportunities for students to review the grammar?

Yes. A Review section is included after every five lessons. These tests can also be used by instructors to measure student understanding of the grammar taught. In addition, there are practice exercises in the Workbook and on the website (elt.thomson.com/grammarconnection).

■ Does *Grammar Connection* assist students in learning new vocabulary?

Yes. The Content Vocabulary section in each lesson of *Grammar Connection* incorporates academic vocabulary building and journaling. In Book 1 this takes a picture dictionary approach. In later books words from the Academic Word List are used. This, along with the content focus, ensures that students expand their vocabulary along with their grammatical capability.

A **picture-based vocabulary** section in lower levels familiarizes students with the content-based academic vocabulary that is used in the lesson. At higher levels, students are introduced to words from the **Academic Word List.**

Grammar Connection is organized into thirty concise lessons, each containing two or three parts of connected grammar points. Every lesson follows a unique pedagogical approach.

Thought-provoking **discussion questions** activate students' knowledge of the content area. The questions can also be used as **diagnostic tests** to assess students' mastery of the grammar before it is taught.

The grammar in each lesson is **contextualized** with topics from different **academic disciplines.**

An integrated **audio program** allows students to listen to the content readings and dialogues.

Content readings and dialogues present the grammar in a meaningful and interesting way.

Contextualized grammar charts provide **easy-to-understand** clear explanations of grammar form as well as notes on usage.

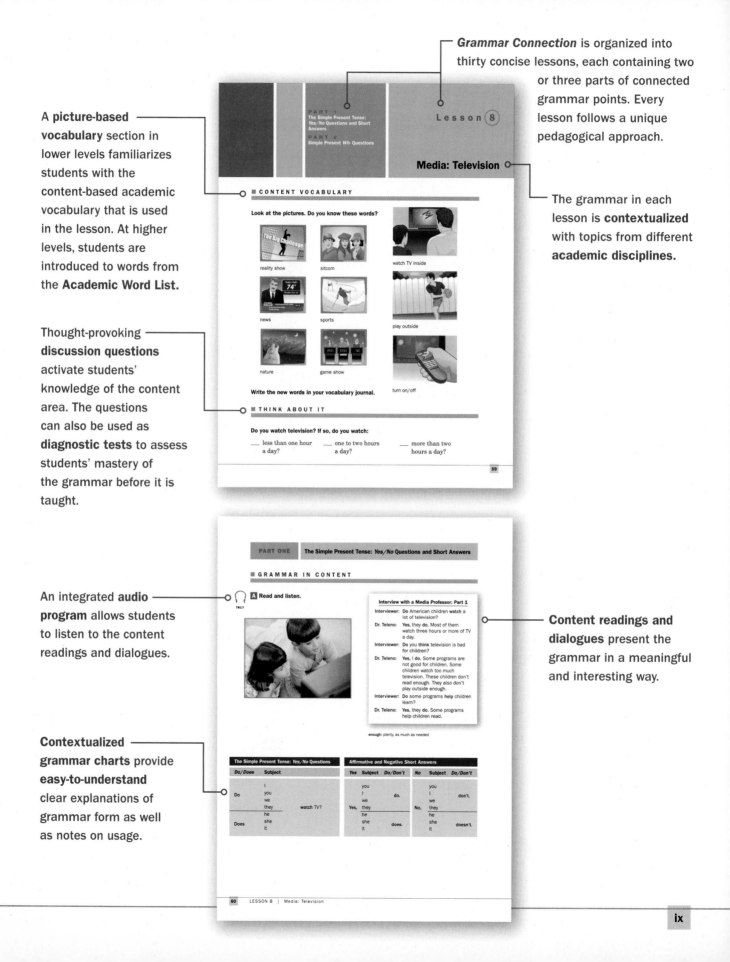

Students move from a variety of controlled exercises to more self-directed ones enabling students to become comfortable using the grammar.

B Look at the dialogue "Interview with a Media Professor: Part 1." Answer the questions with short answers.

1. Do American children watch a lot of television? _____
2. Do they watch one hour of TV a day? _____
3. Do they watch three hours of TV a day? _____
4. Does Dr. Teleno think television is bad for children _____
5. Do some programs help children learn? _____

C PAIR WORK Answer the questions about yourself. Use
your partner the questions. Complete the chart with sh

	Me
1. Do you like television?	
2. Do you watch the news?	
3. Do you watch sitcoms?	
4. Do you watch reality shows?	
5. Do you eat dinner with the television on?	
6. Do you study with the television on?	
7. Do you watch too much television?	

D Put the words in the correct order.

1. at night / you / do / watch television   Do you wa
2. no / don't / I _____ , _____
3. send e-mails / you / do / at night _____
4. don't / no / I _____ , _____
5. study / do / at night / you _____
6. I / do / yes _____ , _____

Part One | The Simple Present Tense: Yes/

---

4. What _____ her son like? _____
5. Where _____ the children watch TV? _____

C Complete the questions. Write *wh-* words.

1. **Q:** _Who_ do you live with? **A:** I live with my husband and son.
2. **Q:** _____ do you study? **A:** I study computer science.
3. **Q:** _____ do you study computer science? **A:** Because I love computers.
4. **Q:** _____ do you relax? **A:** I watch television.
5. **Q:** _____ do you watch? **A:** I watch reality TV programs.
6. **Q:** _____ does your husband work? **A:** He works in an office.
7. **Q:** _____ does he relax? **A:** He reads the newspaper and watches the news.
8. **Q:** _____ does your son watch on TV? **A:** He watches cartoons.

D Complete the dialogue. Write *wh-* questions.

A: There's an interesting program on TV. It's about kangaroos.
B: Really? _Where do kangaroos live_ ?
  (1)
A: Kangaroos live in Australia, Tasmania, and New Guinea.
B: _____ ?
  (2)
A: They eat grass and leaves.
B: _____ ?
  (3)
A: They eat in the late afternoon and early evening.
B: _____ during the day?
  (4)
A: During the day they rest in the shade.
B: _____ get from one place to another?
  (5)
A: They hop!
B: _____ communicate?
  (6)
A: They thump their feet.

64 LESSON 8 | Media: Television

"Communicate" sections allow students to speak or write about their thoughts and experiences.

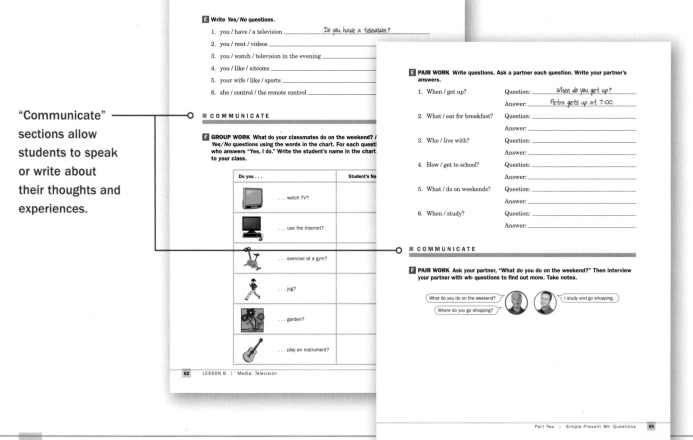

E Write *Yes/No* questions.

1. you / have / a television   _Do you have a television?_
2. you / rent / videos _____
3. you / watch / television in the evening _____
4. you / like / sitcoms _____
5. your wife / like / sports _____
6. she / control / the remote control _____

■ **COMMUNICATE**

F GROUP WORK What do your classmates do on the weekend? A
Yes/No questions using the words in the chart. For each questi
who answers "Yes, I do." Write the student's name in the chart.
to your class.

Do you . . .	Student's Na
. . . watch TV?	
. . . use the Internet?	
. . . exercise at a gym?	
. . . jog?	
. . . garden?	
. . . play an instrument?	

62 LESSON 8 | Media: Television

E PAIR WORK Write questions. Ask a partner each question. Write your partner's answers.

1. When / get up?   Question: _When do you get up?_
      Answer: _Petra gets up at 7:00._
2. What / eat for breakfast? Question: _____
      Answer: _____
3. Who / live with?   Question: _____
      Answer: _____
4. How / get to school?   Question: _____
      Answer: _____
5. What / do on weekends? Question: _____
      Answer: _____
6. When / study?   Question: _____
      Answer: _____

■ **COMMUNICATE**

F PAIR WORK Ask your partner, "What do you do on the weekend?" Then interview your partner with *wh-* questions to find out more. Take notes.

What do you do on the weekend?   I study and go shopping.
Where do you go shopping?

Part Two | Simple Present *Wh-* Questions 65

At the end of each lesson, students are encouraged to put together the **grammar and vocabulary** from the lesson in a productive way.

Interesting projects allow students to put newly learned grammatical forms and vocabulary to use in ways that encourage additional independent reading, **research,** and/or communication. Many of these activities are group activities, further requiring students to put their language skills to work.

Internet activities encourage students to connect the grammar with online resources.

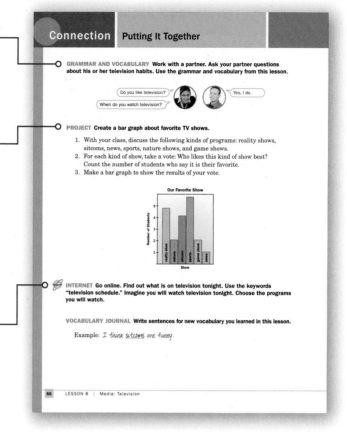

A Review section after every five lessons helps assess and reinforce language learning.

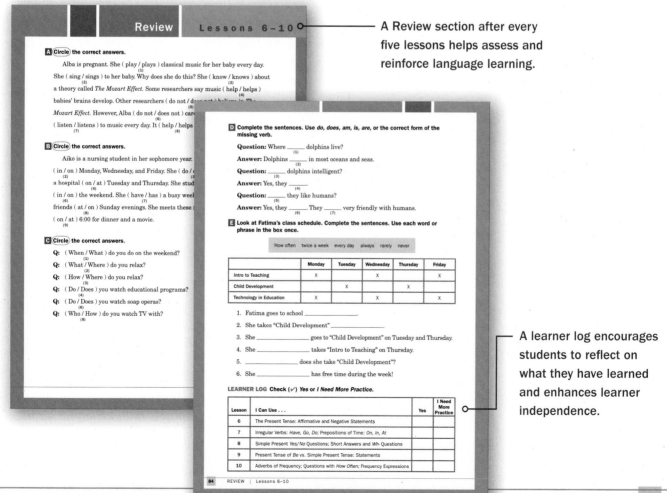

A learner log encourages students to reflect on what they have learned and enhances learner independence.

Supplements

■ Audio Program

Audio CDs and Audio Tapes allow students to listen to every reading in the book to build listening skills and fluency.

■ Workbook

The workbooks review and practice all the grammar points in the Student Book. In addition each workbook includes six Writing Tutorials and vocabulary expansion exercises.

■ Website

Features additional grammar practice activities, vocabulary test items, and other resources: elt.thomson.com/grammarconnection.

■ Annotated Teacher's Edition with Presentation Tool CD-ROM

Offers comprehensive lesson planning advice and teaching tips, as well as a full answer key. The Presentation Tool CD-ROM includes a PowerPoint presentation for selected lessons and includes all the grammar charts from the book.

■ Assessment CD-ROM with ExamView® Pro Test Generator

The customizable generator features lesson, review, mid-term, and term-end assessment items to monitor student progress.

Grammar Connection is based on scientific research on the most effective means of teaching grammar to adult learners of English.

■ Discourse-based Grammar

Research by Celce-Murcia and Olshtain (2000) suggests that learners should go beyond sentence-level exercises in order to use grammar as a resource for comprehending and producing academic discourse. *Grammar Connection* lets students move from controlled exercises to more self-expressive and self-directed ones.

■ Communicative Grammar

Research shows that communicative exercises should complement traditional exercises (Comeau, 1987; Herschensohn, 1988). *Grammar Connection* balances effective controlled activities, such as fill-in-the blanks, with meaningful interactive exercises.

■ Learner-centered Content

Van Duzer (1999) emphasizes that research on adult English language learners shows that "learners should read texts that meet their needs and are interesting." In *Grammar Connection* the content readings are carefully selected and adapted to be both high-interest and relevant to the needs of learners.

■ Vocabulary Development

A number of recent studies have shown the effectiveness of helping English language learners develop independent skills in vocabulary development (Nation, 1990, 2001; Nist & Simpson, 2001; Schmitt, 2000). In *Grammar Connection*, care has been taken to introduce useful academic vocabulary, based in part on Coxhead's (2000) work.

■ Using Background Knowledge

Because research shows that background knowledge facilitates comprehension (Eskey, 1997), each lesson of *Grammar Connection* opens with a "Think About It" section related to the lesson theme.

■ Student Interaction

Learning is enhanced when students work with each other to co-construct knowledge (Grennon-Brooks & Brooks, 1993; Sutherland & Bonwell, 1996). *Grammar Connection* includes many pair and group work exercises as well as interactive projects.

■ References

Celce-Murcia, M., & Olshtain, E. (2000). *Discourse and Context in Language Teaching.* New York: Cambridge University Press.

Comeau, R. Interactive Oral Grammar Exercises. In W. M. Rivers (Ed.), *Interactive Language Teaching* (57–69). Cambridge: Cambridge University Press, 1987.

Coxhead, A. (2000). "A New Academic Word List." *TESOL Quarterly,* 34 (2), 213–238.

Eskey, D. (1997). "Models of Reading and the ESOL Student." *Focus on Basics 1 (B),* 9–11.

Grennon Brooks, J., & Brooks, M. G. (1993). *In Search of Understanding: The Case for Constructivist Classrooms.* Alexandria, VA: Association for Supervision and Curriculum Development.

Herschensohn, J. (1988). "Linguistic Accuracy of Textbook Grammar." *Modern Language Journal 72(4),* 409–414.

Nation, I. S. P. (2001). *Learning Vocabulary in Another Language.* New York: Cambridge University Press.

Nation, I. S. P. (1990). *Teaching and Learning Vocabulary.* Boston: Thomson Heinle.

Nist, S. L., & Simpson, M. L. (2001). *Developing Vocabulary for College Thinking.* Boston: Allyn & Bacon.

Schmitt, N. (2000). *Vocabulary in Language Teaching.* New York: Cambridge University Press.

Sutherland, T. E., & Bonwell, C. C. (Eds.). (1996). "Using Active Learning in College Classes: A Range of Options for Faculty." *New Directions for Teaching and Learning, Number 67,* Fall 1996. San Francisco, CA: Jossey-Bass Publishers.

VanDuzer, C. (1999). "Reading and the Adult Language Learner." *ERIC Digest.* Washington, D.C.: National Center for ESL Literacy Education.

Many thanks to the Thomson ELT team, especially Tom Jefferies and Jim Brown, for their guidance, insight, hard work, and good humor.

This book is dedicated to Mike and Anna—for their love and support, and for keeping me sane and laughing through it all.

— *Jill Korey O'Sullivan*

The author, series editors, and publisher wish to thank the following people for their contributions:

Susan Alexandre
Trimble Technical High School
Fort Worth, TX

Joan Amore
Triton College
River Grove, IL

Cally Andriotis-Williams
Newcomers High School
Long Island City, NY

Ana Maria Cepero
Miami Dade College
Miami, FL

Jacqueline Cunningham
Harold Washington College
Chicago, IL

Kathleen Flynn
Glendale Community College
Glendale, CA

Sally Gearhart
Santa Rosa Junior College
Santa Rosa, CA

Janet Harclerode
Santa Monica College
Santa Monica, CA

Carolyn Ho
North Harris College
Houston, TX

Eugenia Krimmel
Lititz, PA

Dana Liebowitz
Palm Beach Central High
  School
Wellington, FL

Shirley Lundblade
Mt. San Antonio College
Walnut, CA

Craig Machado
Norwalk Community College
Norwalk, CT

Myo Myint
Mission College
Santa Clara, CA

Myra Redman
Miami Dade College
Miami, FL

Eric Rosenbaum
BEGIN Managed Programs
New York, NY

Marilyn Santos
Valencia Community College
Valencia, FL

Laura Sicola
University of Pennsylvania
Philadelphia, PA

Barbara Smith-Palinkas
University of South Florida
Tampa, FL

Kathy Sucher
Santa Monica College
Santa Monica, CA

Patricia Turner
San Diego City College
San Diego, CA

America Vasquez
Miami Dade College, Inter-
  American Campus
Miami, FL

Tracy von Mulaski
El Paso Community College
El Paso, TX

Jane Wang
Mt. San Antonio College
Walnut, CA

Lucy Watel
City College of Chicago - Harry
  S. Truman College
Chicago, IL

Donald Weasenforth
Collin County Community
  College
Plano, TX

PART 1
Parts of Speech

PART 2
Classroom Instructions

PART 3
Vocabulary Journal

Pre-Lesson

Orientation

PART ONE	Parts of Speech

■ NOUNS

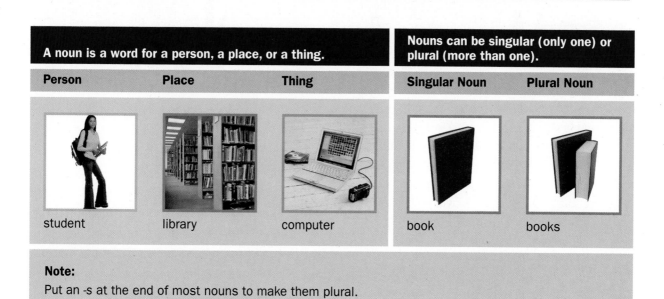

A noun is a word for a person, a place, or a thing.

Person	Place	Thing
student	library	computer

Nouns can be singular (only one) or plural (more than one).

Singular Noun	Plural Noun
book	books

Note:
Put an -s at the end of most nouns to make them plural.

A Write the singular or plural noun.

Singular	Plural		Singular	Plural
1. book	_books_	4. _____		doors
2. _____	windows	5. computer		_____
3. student	_____	6. _____		chairs

B (Circle) the noun.

1. (a teacher)	happy	sit	4. fast	on	a desk
2. read	a book	big	5. work	a mother	up
3. study	green	a school	6. small	a house	eat

■ SUBJECT PRONOUNS

The subject pronouns are *I, you, he, she, it, we,* and *they.*

Singular Subject Pronouns	Plural Subject Pronouns

I   you   we   you

he   she   it   they

Notes:
- Subject pronouns take the place of nouns. For example:

  Mother is at home. = *She* is at home.

  John and Susan are in class. = *They* are in class.
- We use *it* to talk about singular objects. We use *they* to talk about plural things.

  The book is on the desk. = *It* is on the desk.

  The books are on the desk. = *They* are on the desk.

C Write a pronoun for the person or thing(s) in the pictures.

1. *he*   2. _____   3. _____

4. _____   5. _____   6. _____

D Write a pronoun for the nouns.

1. The pen _it_
2. The man _____
3. Mary _____
4. David _____
5. David and Mary _____
6. David and I _____

7. The dictionary _____
8. The chairs _____
9. The chair _____
10. My mother _____
11. My parents _____
12. The school _____

■ VERBS

Verbs are "action" words.

talk   write

Verbs also tell about feelings, states, or conditions.

love   think

E Circle the verb in each group.

1. a home	(walk)	she	4. talk	a telephone	on
2. study	good	a student	5. a book	read	big
3. a pen	blue	write	6. chocolate	I	love

F PAIR WORK Choose a verb. Perform the verb for your partner. Your partner will guess the verb. Take turns.

Adjectives describe nouns.			

happy

sad

large

small

Note:
Adjectives come before nouns. Example: *small desk*

G (Circle) **the adjective in each group.**

1. on   (blue)   a backpack
2. sit   a chair   large
3. new   buy   shoes

4. a book   carry   heavy
5. nice   a friend   she
6. a teacher   difficult   homework

H **Match the opposites.**

1. _c_ new   a. cheap

2. ___ expensive   b. closed

3. ___ black   c. old

4. ___ open   d. white

5. ___ fast   e. slow

I **Complete the sentences.**

1. I have a new _____.

2. I have an old _____.

3. I have an expensive _____.

4. I have a cheap _____.

5. I have a white _____.

6. I have a black _____.

read

listen

What's your name?
My name is Kaito.
ask   answer

I think that . . .
I think . . .
discuss

Instruction	Example
Underline the adjective.	I have a <u>new</u> dictionary.
Circle the verb.	You (work) in a school.
Fill in the blank.	She _____is_____ a teacher.
Complete the sentence.	I speak _____Spanish and English._____
Match the items.	1. _b_ noun a. new 2. _a_ adjective b. book
Correct the sentence.	I is a student. ^am
Choose the correct answer.	They (is / (are)) my friends.
Check (✔) the correct answer.	English is a country. ____ English is a language. ✔
Put the words in order.	from are We China. _We are from China._
Write a sentence.	_I am a student._
Write a paragraph.	_I am a student. I study history. One day I want to be a history professor at a university._

A **Match the items.**

1. _b_ listen   a. noun

2. ___ instructor   b. verb

3. ___ small   c. pronoun

4. ___ she   d. adjective

B <u>Underline</u> the nouns.

<u>a clock</u>   listen   white   a teacher   happy   run   a backpack

C (Circle) the verbs.

(read)   a book   a house   eat   old   talk   expensive

D Check (✔) the correct answers.

1. "a cat" is: <u>✔</u> a noun   ___ a verb

2. "eat" is: ___ a noun   ___ a verb

3. "happy" is: ___ a verb   ___ an adjective

4. "they" is: ___ an adjective ___ a pronoun

E Correct the sentences.

1. "An instructor" is a ~~verb~~.   3. "It" is an adjective.
                     ^
2. "Eat" is a noun.   *noun*   4. "Happy" is a pronoun.

PART THREE   Vocabulary Journal

In this textbook you will learn a lot of new vocabulary. Use a vocabulary journal to help you learn these new words. To create a vocabulary journal you should:

1. Write a letter of the alphabet at the top of each page.
2. Write new words in your vocabulary journal under the correct letter.
3. Draw a picture or write a definition and a sentence using each word.
4. Study the words every evening.

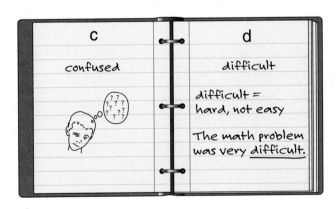

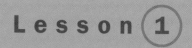

College Success: First Day

■ CONTENT VOCABULARY

Look at the picture. Do you know these words?

class

Write the new words in your vocabulary journal.

■ THINK ABOUT IT

Check (✔) the statements you agree with.

1. On the first day of class, students are often:

   excited ___   nervous ___   happy ___   confused ___

2. My school is big. ___   My school is old. ___

   The instructors are good. ___   The classes are interesting. ___

■ GRAMMAR IN CONTENT

TR1

A Read and listen.

First Day of College

My name **is** Bella. I **am** from Mexico. Today **is** my first day at college. I'**m** excited. I'**m** also nervous. It is 1:30 now. I **am** in Chemistry 105. The students **are** nice. They **are** from different countries. Mr. Frank **is** the instructor. He'**s** nice, too.

countries: for example: Mexico, Japan, Australia

The Present Tense of *Be*: Affirmative Statements			Contraction			*Be* + Adjective		
Subject	*Be*		Contraction			Subject	*Be*	Adjective
I	am	a student.	I'm		a student.	I	am	happy.
He She It	is	from China.	He's She's It's		from China.	He She It	is	tall.
You We They	are	in class.	You're We're They're		in class.	You We They	are	Brazilian.

Notes:

- Use *be*:
    1. to say what someone or something is. Example: *I am a student.*
    2. to describe someone or something. Example: *I am nervous.*
    3. to talk about where someone or something is. Example: *I am in class.*
    4. to talk about where someone is from. Example: *I am from Mexico.*
    5. to talk about age. Example: *I am 25.*
    6. with *it* to talk about weather or time. Example: *It is 2:45.*
- Contractions are used in informal speech and writing.
- *You* is both singular and plural.

B Look at the reading "First Day of College." (Circle) the correct form of *be.*

1. Bella (am / (is)) a student.
2. She says, "I (am / is) excited."
3. It (is / are) the first day of college.
4. The students (is / are) nice.
5. They (am / are) from many different countries.
6. Mr. Frank (am / is) her instructor.

C Complete the paragraph. Use *am, is,* or *are.*

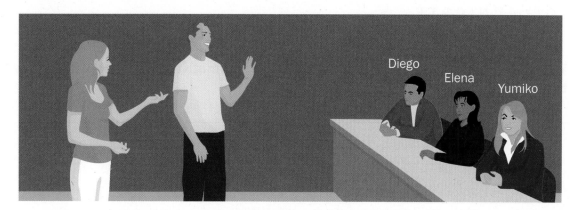

Welcome to English 103! I __am__ Julia Marks. I _____ the instructor. Class,
                        (1)   (2)

this is Ivan. He _____ from Russia. We _____ happy to meet you, Ivan. Please
                 (3)   (4)

sit with Yumiko, Diego, and Elena. They _____ excellent students. Yumiko
                                        (5)

_____ a computer science student. She _____ from Japan. Diego and Elena
(6)   (7)

_____ from South America. Diego _____ from Columbia. He _____ a biology
(8)   (9)   (10)

student. Elena _____ from Brazil. She _____ a nursing student. You _____
               (11)   (12)   (13)

lucky. You _____ in a great class. The students _____ nice. And the teacher
          (14)   (15)

_____ excellent.
(16)

D Rewrite the sentences. Use contractions.

1. She is a biology student. _____*She's a biology student.*_____

2. I am 23. _____

3. They are from China. _____

4. He is nervous. _____

5. We are in room 208. _____

6. It is 4:15. _____

E **Write about yourself.**

1. I _____ (what kind of student you are)

2. I _____ (your age)

3. I _____ (country you are from)

4. I _____ (how you feel)

5. I _____ (where you are now)

■ **C O M M U N I C A T E**

F **WRITE** Write about yourself and a friend. Use affirmative sentences with *be.* Use the vocabulary from this lesson.

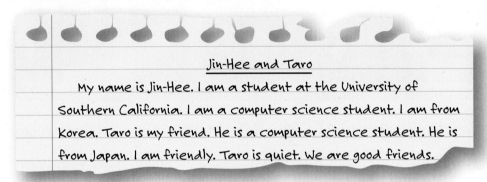

<u>Jin-Hee and Taro</u>

My name is Jin-Hee. I am a student at the University of Southern California. I am a computer science student. I am from Korea. Taro is my friend. He is a computer science student. He is from Japan. I am friendly. Taro is quiet. We are good friends.

PART TWO	The Present Tense of *Be*: Negative Statements

■ **G R A M M A R   I N   C O N T E N T**

TR2

A **Read and listen.**

Wrong Class

Instructor: Hola!

Student: Professor Davidson?

Instructor: No. I **am not** Professor Davidson. I am Professor Ortiz.

Student: I'm confused. Is this English 205?

Instructor: No, it **isn't**. It's Spanish 311. You **are not** in the right class.

Student: Oh. You're right! **I'm not** in the right class. Sorry!

Instructor: Adiós!

Hola: Spanish for "hello"   **Adiós:** Spanish for "goodbye"

The Present Tense of *Be*: Negative Statements

Subject	*Be* + not		Contraction			
I	**am not**	a student.	I**'m not** a student.			
He She It	**is not**	from Mexico.	He She It	**isn't** **isn't** **isn't**	(OR: He**'s not**) (OR: She**'s not**) (OR: It**'s not**)	from Mexico.
You We They	**are not**	happy.	You We They	**aren't** **aren't** **aren't**	(OR: You**'re not**) (OR: We**'re not**) (OR: They**'re not**)	happy.

Note:
There is no contraction for *am not*.

B Look at the reading "Wrong Class." (Circle) the correct answers.

1. Professor Ortiz (is / (is not)) an English instructor.
2. He (is / is not) a Spanish instructor.
3. The student (is / is not) confused.
4. Professor Ortiz says: You (are / are not) in the right class.
5. The student (is / is not) in the right class.

C Complete the sentences about yourself. Use the correct affirmative or negative form of *be.*

1. I ____*am not*____ an English instructor.

2. I _____ a college student.

3. Today _____ Wednesday.

4. It _____ the first day of college.

5. My instructor _____ a man.

6. My classmates _____ American.

D Rewrite the sentences. Use the negative contraction of *be.*

1. She is an instructor.   (student) _____ *She isn't a student.* _____

2. You are late.   (early) _____

3. It is 8:00.   (9:00) _____

4. He is a good student.   (bad) _____

5. They are happy.   (sad) _____

E PAIR WORK Say true and false sentences. Use *be.* Take turns.

We are in class.

Mr. Harris is from Peru.

Right!

Wrong! Mr. Harris isn't from Peru. He's from the United States.

Connection | Putting It Together

GRAMMAR AND VOCABULARY Work in a group. Write true sentences about yourself. Use the grammar and vocabulary from this lesson. Put all of the papers in a pile. Each student in the group takes a turn reading one of the papers out loud. The group will listen and guess who the student is.

About Me

1. I am an engineering student.

2. I am not from China.

3. I am happy.

4. I am very nice!

PROJECT Create a class book.

1. Work in groups of three students.
2. Write a page about the students in your group. Include photos.
3. Put your pages together with the other groups' pages to make a class book.

About Us

Yolanda is 25 years old. She's from Mexico. Latifa is Saudi Arabian. She is nervous about her first day at school. Chen is from China. He is a music student. We are an interesting group.

 INTERNET Go online. Use the keywords "advice," "first day," and "student." Find an interesting article. Share a piece of advice from the article with your class.

VOCABULARY JOURNAL Write sentences for new vocabulary you learned in this lesson.

Example: I am <u>nervous</u> before tests.

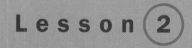

P A R T 1
The Present Tense of *Be*:
Yes/No Questions and Short
Answers

P A R T 2
The Present Tense of *Be*:
Wh- Questions

College Success: Filling Out Forms

■ CONTENT VOCABULARY

Look at the picture and form. Do you know the words?

fill out

Student Registration Form

Name   Smith   Derek
    (Last name)   (First name)

Date of birth   5/12/63   Sex   Male ✔

Telephone number   (305)555-4598   Female

Address   53 Tampa Street
    Miami, FL 33245

E-mail address   dsmith@site.net

Social security number   543-XX-1138

Signature   *Derek Smith*   Date   9/15/06

Write the new words in your vocabulary journal.

■ THINK ABOUT IT

1. **What information is on Derek's form? Check (✔) the boxes.**

   ☐ name   ☐ sex   ☐ eye color   ☐ date of birth
   ☐ age   ☐ favorite food   ☐ address   ☐ signature

2. **What forms do you fill out at college? Discuss with a partner.**

Lesson ②

■ GRAMMAR IN CONTENT

TR3

A **Read and listen.**

The Registration Form (Part 1)

Igor: Is this the history department office?

Stacy: Yes, it is. Are you a new student?

Igor: Yes, I am. My name is Igor. I'm Russian.

Stacy: Welcome, Igor. I'm Stacy. Here is a new student registration form.

Igor: Um . . . thanks.

Stacy: Are you OK?

Igor: Well . . . no, I'm not. This form is confusing.

Stacy: No problem. I can help you.

Igor: Great. Thanks!

confusing: not clear; hard to understand

help: assist; support

The Present Tense of *Be: Yes/No* Questions		
Be	Subject	
Am	I	right?
Is	he she it	a student?
Are	you we they	tired?

Note:
Yes/No questions only ask for *Yes/No* answers.

Short Answers with *Be*					
Affirmative			**Negative**		
	Subject	*Be*		Subject + *Be* + *Not*	
Yes,	I	am.	No,	I'm not.	
	he she it	is.		he **isn't.** OR he's **not.** she **isn't.** OR she's **not.** it **isn't.** OR it's **not.**	
	you we they	are.		you **aren't.** OR you're **not.** we **aren't.** OR we're **not.** they **aren't.** OR they're **not.**	

Note:
Do not contract forms of *be* after *yes*.
Example: *Yes, I am.* (NOT: *Yes, I'm.*)

B **Look at the dialogue "The Registration Form (Part 1)." <u>Underline</u> the questions with *be*. (Circle) the short answers.**

C Look at the dialogue "The Registration Form (Part 1)." (Circle) the correct short answers.

1. Are Igor and Stacy in a classroom?   Yes, they are. / (No, they aren't.)
2. Are they in the history department office? Yes, they are. / No, they aren't.
3. Is Igor a new student?   Yes, he is.   / No, he isn't.
4. Is the registration form confusing for Igor? Yes, it is.   / No, it isn't.
5. Is Spanish Igor's first language?   Yes, it is.   / No, it isn't.

D Look at the student ID cards. Answer the questions.

Wilmington University
Student ID
Name: **Yan Lu**
Date of Birth: **3/5/87**
Student ID Number: **10023**

City College
Student ID
Name: **Antonio Rios**
Date of Birth: **4/9/53**
Student ID Number: **10345**

1. Are Yan and Antonio instructors? _____ *No, they aren't.* _____

2. Are they students? _____

3. Is Yan 20 years old? _____

4. Is her student ID number 10023? _____

5. Is Antonio's birthday April 9? _____

6. Is his student ID number 10045? _____

7. Is he a City College student? _____

E Write short answers to the questions.

1. Are you a teacher? _____

2. Are you from the United States? _____

3. Are you a science student? _____

4. Are you in class now? _____

F **PAIR WORK** Ask your partner the questions in exercise E. Write down his or her answers. Tell your class about your partner.

G Listen. Complete the conversation.

TR4

1. **Instructor:** _____ _____ an art student?
      (1)   (2)

   Herman: Yes, I _____.
                        (3)

2. **Akiko:** _____ she a biology student?
                (4)

   Sofia: _____, _____ _____.
               (5)   (6)   (7)

3. **Ricardo:** _____ _____ professors?
                  (8)   (9)

   Toshi: _____, _____ not.
               (10)   (11)

4. **Yang-sook:** _____ _____ 10:30?
                      (12)   (13)

   Instructor Jones: _____, _____ _____.
                          (14)   (15)   (16)

H Write *Yes / No* questions.

1. your school / large _____ *Is your school large?* _____

2. English / difficult _____

3. your instructor / nice _____

4. this class / interesting _____

5. you / tired today _____

■ COMMUNICATE

I PAIR WORK Ask your partner the questions from exercise H.

J GROUP WORK Work in groups of four students. One student thinks of a famous person. The other students ask *Yes/No* questions with *be.* Guess the person. Take turns.

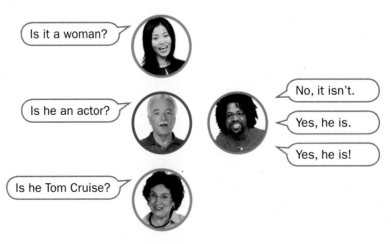

Is it a woman?

Is he an actor?

No, it isn't.

Yes, he is.

Yes, he is!

Is he Tom Cruise?

■ GRAMMAR IN CONTENT

TR5

A Read and listen.

The Registration Form (Part 2)

Stacy: **What is** your name?

Igor: Igor Petrov.

Stacy: OK. Write it here. **What's** your date of birth?

Igor: It's January 8, 1973. Excuse me, **what** time is it?

Stacy: It's 10:15.

Igor: Oh no! I'm late for class.

Stacy: **When's** your class?

Igor: 10:00.

Stacy: **Where's** your class?

Igor: It's in the Johnson building.

Stacy: **Who's** the instructor?

Igor: Mr. Craig.

Stacy: You should go to your class. We can fill out the form later.

Igor: OK. Thanks.

---

late: not on time

The Present Tense of *Be*: *Wh-* Questions

Meaning of *Wh-* Words	*Wh-* Word	*Be*	Subject	Answer		
who — people	Who	are	they?	My friends.	OR	They are my friends.
what — things	What	is	your name?	Eduardo.	OR	My name is Eduardo.
where — places	Where	is	the office?	Room 205.	OR	It's in Room 205.
when — time	When	is	the exam?	May 25.	OR	It's May 25.
how — description	How	are	you?	Fine.	OR	I'm fine.

Notes:

• *Wh-* words ask for information.

• You can make the following contractions with *wh-* words: *What is* = *What's*, *Where is* = *Where's*, *How is* = *How's*, *Who is* = *Who's*, *When is* = *When's*.

B Look at the dialogue "The Registration Form (Part 2)." (Circle) the correct answers.

1. What is the student's name?   a. a student   (b.) Igor   c. Mr. Craig
2. What is the student's date of birth?   a. 1/8/73   b. the office   c. 132 Brent Avenue
3. What is the problem?   a. He's late.   b. Igor   c. Russian
4. When is the class?   a. 10:00   b. 5:00   c. Mr. Craig
5. Where is the class?   a. the Johnson building   b. Russia   c. 132 Post Street
6. Who is the instructor?   a. Mr. Craig   b. Stacy   c. history

C Look at the student registration form. Match the questions to the correct answers.

Student Registration Form

Name   Vargas   Marina
        (Last name)   (First name)

Date of birth   5/12/84   Sex   Male _____

Telephone number   (310) 555-4598   Female   ✓

Address   53 Danvers Street
       Los Angeles, CA 90012

E-mail address   mvargas@site.net

Social security number   134-XX-7889

Signature   Marina Vargas   Date   9/3/06

_h_ 1. What is her first name?

____ 2. What is the date?

____ 3. What is her date of birth?

____ 4. What is her last name?

____ 5. What is her address?

____ 6. What is her e-mail address?

____ 7. What is her telephone number?

____ 8. What is her social security number?

a. Vargas
b. 9/3/06
c. 134-XX-7889
d. 5/12/84
e. (310) 555-4598
f. 53 Danvers Street, Los Angeles, CA 90012
g. mvargas@site.net
h. Marina

D Complete the questions. Use a *wh-* word.

1. ___What___ is your name?   John.

2. _____ is your instructor?   Ms. Smith.

3. _____ is the class?   Biology 205.

4. _____ is the test?   It's tomorrow.

5. _____ are the students?   Very smart.

6. _____ is the class?   It's in the science building.

E Read the dialogue. Write *wh-* questions.

Doric: Hi! (What) _____ What is your name? _____
                                                    (1)

Tom: My name is Tom Davison. What's yours?

Doric: Doric. (Who) _____
                                            (2)

Tom: Mr. Delgado is my English instructor. He's nice.

Doric: (How) _____
                                    (3)

Tom: My classes are very interesting. I like them. Oh! I have to go. I have an appointment with Mr. Delgado.

Doric: (When) _____
                                      (4)

Tom: It's at 12:30. See you!

■ COMMUNICATE

F **WRITE** Write five *wh-* questions to ask your teacher. Then ask the questions and write the answers.

Interview Questions for My Teacher
1. What is your first name?
2. Where are you from?
3. When is the final exam?

GRAMMAR AND VOCABULARY Write five more questions. Use the grammar and vocabulary from this lesson. Ask three of your classmates the questions. Write their answers.

Question	Classmate #1	Classmate #2	Classmate #3
What's your name?			
Are you a nursing student?			

PROJECT Create a school quiz.

1. Work with a group.
2. With your group, think of *Yes/No* and *wh-* questions to ask about your school.
3. Find out the answers to the questions. Look through the school catalog and ask staff members questions.
4. Create a multiple-choice exam about your school.
5. Give the test to the other groups.

```
                    School Quiz

   1. Who is the President of our University?
   a) Ann Lawrence   b) Alan Brown

   2. Is the library in the Johnson Building?
   a) Yes, it is.   b) No, it isn't.

   3. What are the school colors?
   a) Red and Blue   b) Brown and Gold
```

 INTERNET Go online. Search for a local college or university. Find admissions information. How do you apply to the college? What forms do you need to fill out? Report back to your class.

VOCABULARY JOURNAL Write sentences for new vocabulary you learned in this lesson.

Example: My date of birth is 9/3/86.

PART 1
Singular and Plural Nouns

PART 2
Spelling and Pronunciation of
Regular Plural Nouns

Lesson ③

College Success:
The Classroom

■ CONTENT VOCABULARY

Look at the picture. Do you know the words?

whiteboard

$$1-I_{ij} = exp\left[-I_{ij}N_{IJ}/N_T\right]$$

door

clock

window

highlighter   eraser

notebook

textbook

table

pencil   pen

chair

Write the new words in your vocabulary journal.

■ THINK ABOUT IT

What's in your classroom? Check (✔) the items you see. Add more items.

☐ a notebook   ☐ a window   ☐ _____
☐ dictionaries ☐ a table
☐ pencils   ☐ a door   ☐ _____
☐ an eraser   ☐ chairs   ☐ _____

☐ _____

■ GRAMMAR IN CONTENT

TR6

A **Read and listen.**

English Composition 101
Instructor: Frank Jackson
Room: Lynn Campus, L430
Time: 9:00–11:00

Please bring these items to class every day:

☑ a notebook   ☑ pens   ☑ a dictionary   ☑ questions!

☑ pencils   ☑ a highlighter   ☑ an eraser

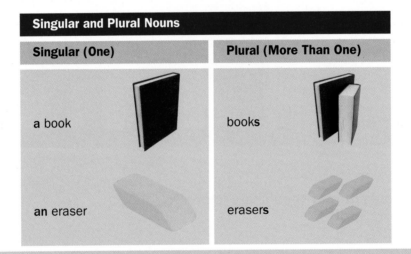

Singular and Plural Nouns	
Singular (One)	**Plural (More Than One)**
a book	books
an eraser	erasers

Notes:
- Use *a* and *an* with singular nouns. Example: *a car, an apple*
- Do not use *a* and *an* with plural nouns. Example: *a cars, an apples*
- Use *a* before nouns that start with a consonant sound like *book, pen,* and *desk.* Use *an* before nouns that start with a vowel sound like *eraser, item,* and *instructor.*
- Put an *-s* at the end of most nouns to make them plural. Example: *one book, two book**s***
- You can put a number before plural nouns: Example: *I have **three** books.*
- Some plural nouns do not end in *-s.* They have irregular plural forms. Common irregular plural nouns are *child/children, foot/feet, man/men, mouse/mice, tooth/teeth,* and *woman/women.*

B **Look at "English Composition 101."** <u>Underline</u> all of the singular nouns. (Circle) all of the plural nouns.

C Write *a* or *an*.

1. _a_ pen   4. ____ table   7. ____ apple   10. ____ college

2. ____ window   5. ____ eraser   8. ____ chair   11. ____ hour

3. ____ elevator   6. ____ door   9. ____ library   12. ____ year

D Write the plural of the nouns.

1. elevator _____ *elevators* _____   4. pen _____

2. apple _____   5. highlighter _____

3. woman _____   6. college _____

E Write a sentence. Use *It's* and a singular noun or *They're* and a plural noun.

1. What is it?

_____ It's a table. _____

2. What are they?

_____

3. What is it?

_____

4. What are they?

_____

5. What are they?

_____

6. What is it?

_____

F **PAIR WORK** Student A closes his or her eyes. Student B chooses one or more items from the box below and puts the item(s) in Student A's hands. Student B says "What is it?" or "What are they?" Student A guesses "It's . . . " or "They're . . . " Take turns.

one or more pens	one or more notebooks
one or more pencils	one or more textbooks
one or more highlighters	one or more erasers

PART TWO	Spelling and Pronunciation of Regular Plural Nouns

■ GRAMMAR IN CONTENT

Spelling of Regular Plural Nouns

Base Form	Plural Form	Rule
book teacher	book**s** teacher**s**	For most plural nouns: Add -s
bus box	bus**es** box**es**	If the noun ends in s, z, x, ch, sh: Add -es
dictionary library	dictionar**ies** librar**ies**	If the noun ends in a consonant + y: Change y to i and add -es
shelf knife	shel**ves** kni**ves**	For some nouns that end in f or fe: Change the f or fe to -ves
photo tomato	phot**os** tomat**oes**	If the noun ends with a consonant + o, some words take -s and others take -es.

A Write the plural form of each noun.

1. computer _computers_

2. student _____

3. dish _____

4. party _____

5. pencil _____

6. leaf _____

7. comedy _____

8. clock _____

9. life _____

B Complete the sentences with the plural form of a word from the box.

city	country	university	~~day~~	class	test

1. Monday and Wednesday are _____ *days* _____.

2. Harvard and Oxford are _____.

3. Biology 203 and English 105 are _____.

4. The TOEFL and the SAT are _____.

5. Japan and Brazil are _____.

6. Tokyo and São Paulo are _____.

Pronunciation of Regular Plural Nouns

There are three ways of pronouncing the final -s and -es.

For Nouns That End in . . .	Pronounce the Third Person -s:
the sounds *f, k, p, t,* or *th*	/s/ as in "books" and "pens"
the sounds *b, d, g, l, m, n, ng, r, v,* and all vowels	/z/ as in "teachers" and "boards"
s, se, ss, sh, ch, ge, ce, and *x*	/əz/ as in "classes" and "colleges"

C Listen. Check (✔) the plural sound you hear at the end of each word.

TR7

	/S/ as in "books"	/Z/ as in "teachers"	/əZ/ as in "classes"
1.			✔
2.			
3.			
4.			
5.			
6.			
7.			
8.			

D **PAIR WORK** First, practice spelling plural nouns: Student A says a plural noun from this lesson and Student B spells the noun. Take turns. Next, practice pronouncing plural nouns: Student A spells a noun from the lesson and Student B says the noun. Take turns.

Connection | Putting It Together

GRAMMAR AND VOCABULARY Work with a partner. Identify the items below. Use the grammar and vocabulary from this lesson.

Next, choose five different classroom items with your partner. Draw pictures of the items. Ask another pair to guess what the pictures are.

PROJECT **Have a spelling bee.**

1. The class works in two groups.
2. Each group chooses ten nouns from this lesson.
3. The groups find objects and/or pictures for each of the nouns. Some of the objects/pictures should show only one of the item, and some should show two or more of the item.
4. A member of Group A holds up one of the objects or pictures.
5. A member of Group B must identify the object(s) correctly using *a / an* or the plural -*s,* then spell the word.
6. If Group B uses *a / an* or -*s* correctly and pronounces and spells the word correctly, they get one point.
7. Take turns. The group with the most points wins.

erasers!

e-r-a-s-e-r-s

 INTERNET Go online. Choose a job you are interested in. What equipment does this job use? Use the name of the job (for example, "artist") and "equipment" as the keywords. Make a list of the items you find. Place *a* or *an* before singular items and make sure there is a plural -*s* at the end of regular plural nouns.

VOCABULARY JOURNAL Write sentences for new vocabulary you learned in this lesson.

Example: *My classroom has six tables.*

College Success: Finding Your Way Around

■ CONTENT VOCABULARY

Look at the pictures. Do you know the words?

give directions

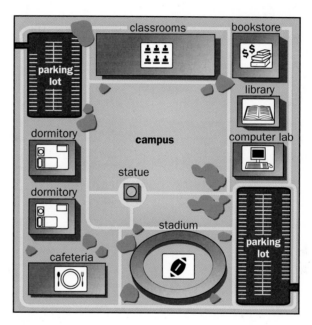

map

Write the new words in your vocabulary journal.

■ THINK ABOUT IT

1. What places are there in your school or college? Write a list with a partner.

   _library,_____

2. Is your school or college large? Are there many buildings? Is it difficult to find your way around? Discuss with a partner.

■ GRAMMAR IN CONTENT

TR8

A **Read and listen.**

Is This Wendell Hall?

Student:	Excuse me. What building is **this**?
Secretary:	**This** is Wendell Hall.
Student:	Is the main office in **this** building?
Secretary:	No. **That**'s across from Stevens Hall.
Student:	**This** campus is confusing!
Secretary:	Take **this**.
Student:	What's **that**?
Secretary:	**This**? It's a map of the campus. Here. Take two.
Student:	Thanks. **These** maps are helpful.

This, That, These, Those

Near Speaker		Not Near Speaker	
Singular			
This is a map. **This** map is helpful.		**That** is a map. **That** map is helpful.	
Plural			
These are maps. **These** maps are helpful.		**Those** are maps. **Those** maps are helpful.	

Notes:
- The contraction for *That is* = *That's*.
- There is no contraction for *This is, These are,* or *Those are*.

B Complete each sentence with *This*, *That*, *These*, or *Those*.

1. ___These___ are textbooks.

2. _____ is a catalog.

3. _____ is the computer lab.

4. _____ are restrooms.

C Complete the sentences. Use *This*, *That*, *These*, or *Those* and *be*.

1. ___This___ ___is___ the bookstore.

2. ___These___ ___are___ the books for your class.

3. _____ _____ the cafeteria.

4. _____ _____ the vending machines.

5. _____ _____ my lunch.

6. Ssshh! _____ _____ the library.

7. _____ _____ the checkout desk.

8. _____ _____ the computers.

9. _____ _____ the football stadium.

10. _____ _____ the bleachers.

11. _____ _____ my ticket for the next game.

D PAIR WORK Student A points to object(s) in class. Student B says what the object(s) is/are. Use *be* and *This, That, These,* or *Those.* Take turns.

That's a clock.

E PAIR WORK Close your eyes. Your partner will put something in your hand. Guess what the object(s) is/are. Use *This is* or *These are.* Take turns.

PART TWO	Prepositions of Location

Prepositions of Location

The dictionary is **on** the desk.

Marco is **in** class.

Marco is **in front of** Jane. Jane is **behind** Marco.

Marco is **next to** Tim.
Marco is **between** Tim and Yuko.

Marco is **across from** the instructor.

Yuko is **near** the door.

A Check (✔) *True* or *False*.

	True	False		True	False
1. I am in class.	☐	☐	5. My instructor is across from me.	☐	☐
2. My pens are on my desk.	☐	☐	6. I am next to the wall.	☐	☐
3. My textbook is in my bag.	☐	☐	7. I am between two students.	☐	☐
4. The whiteboard is behind me.	☐	☐	8. I am in front of a male student.	☐	☐

B Look at the picture. Complete the sentences. Use prepositions of location.

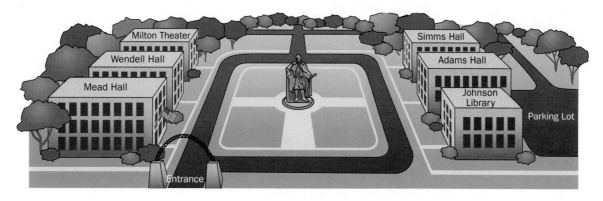

1. Simms Hall is ___next to___ Adams Hall.

2. Mead Hall is _____ the entrance.

3. The flag is _____ Mead Hall.

4. The statue is _____ the courtyard.

5. Adams Hall is _____ Wendell Hall.

6. Johnson Library is _____ the parking lot.

7. Wendell Hall is _____ Mead Hall and the Milton Theater.

8. The parking lot is _____ the library.

■ **COMMUNICATE**

C **PAIR WORK** Work with a partner. One partner describes the location of a partner, using prepositions of location. The other partner guesses the person. Take turns.

He is between Mika and Irina. He is behind Carlo. He is in front of me.

It's Pavel!

D WRITE Choose a place you know (for example, the town where you live or your campus). Write about it. Use prepositions of location. Tell your class about the place.

My House

I live in Springfield. I like my house. It is small. It has three rooms. My house is next to a store. It is also across from a park.

Connection | Putting It Together

GRAMMAR AND VOCABULARY Choose a place on your campus or in your school. Pretend you are giving a tour of this place to a new student. Explain where to find different things in this place. Your classmates will guess the place. Use the grammar and vocabulary from this lesson.

Those are the dictionaries. The notebooks are next to the dictionaries. ESL books are on that shelf. The cashier is near the door.

You are in the bookstore!

PROJECT Create a map of your school.

1. Work in small groups.
2. Discuss the different buildings and offices on your campus.
3. Draw an outline of the buildings and offices. Make sure everyone in your group agrees on the locations.
4. Use the outline to draw a map of your school on a large poster.
5. Present your map to the class. Talk about the places in your school.
6. The other students will tell your group if anything on your map is in the wrong place.

 INTERNET Go online. Find a map of your campus or town. Print it out. Show it to your class and talk about the map.

VOCABULARY JOURNAL Write sentences for new vocabulary you learned in this lesson.

Example: *There are many books in the library.*

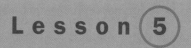

College Success: People and Programs

■ CONTENT VOCABULARY

Look at the pictures. Do you know the words?

Thomson University
Admissions Office

Click below to find more information on the courses at Thomson University.

art

business

computer science

engineering

nursing

undergraduate: a student in any of the first four years of college

international: a student who is not from the country in which he or she is going to school

part-time: a student who is taking less than a full course load

full-time: a student who is taking a full course load

Write the new words in your vocabulary journal.

■ THINK ABOUT IT

1. How many students are there at your school or college? (Circle) the closest number.

   10   100   1,000   10,000   20,000

2. How many students are there in your class? Circle the closest number.

   5   10   25   50   100

3. Are there more men or more women in your class? Circle your answer.

   more men   more women

■ GRAMMAR IN CONTENT

A **Read and listen.**

TR9

A World-Famous University

Harvard University is a famous American university. It is in Cambridge, Massachusetts. Here are some facts about the university.

- **There are** 6,562 students in the undergraduate school.
- **There are** 545 international students.
- **There are** 40 programs for undergraduate students. **There are** programs in mathematics, chemistry, art, languages, and sociology.
- **There is** a waiting list for most classes.
- **There is** a final examination for every class.

famous: very well known
examination: test

There Is/There Are		
Singular		
There + is	**Subject**	**Location**
There is	a nursing program	at my college.
There is	one library	on campus.
Plural		
There + are	**Subject**	**Location**
There are	ten students	in my class.
There are	some books	on the desk.

Notes:
- The contraction for *there is* is *there's*. There is no contraction for *there are*.
- An adjective can be placed before either a singular or a plural noun. Example: *There is an **excellent** college in this city. There are **excellent** colleges in this city.*
- Don't confuse *there are* and *they are*.

B Look at the reading "A World-Famous University." ⟨Circle⟩ the right answers.

1. (There is /⟨There are⟩) 40 programs for undergraduate students.
2. (There is / There are) 6,562 students in the undergraduate school.
3. (There is / There are) 545 international students.
4. (There is / There are) a final exam for each course.

C Look at the pie chart. Complete the sentences.

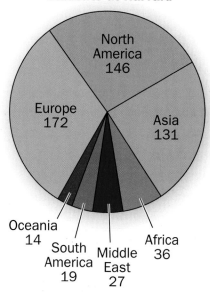

International Undergraduate Students at Harvard

1. _____There are 27 students_____ from the Middle East.

2. _____ from Africa.

3. _____ from Europe.

4. _____ from Oceania.

5. _____ from North America.

6. _____ from South America.

7. _____ from Asia.

8. _____ international

undergraduate students at Harvard.

D Write sentences. Use *There is* and *There are.*

1. 7,000 students / at his college ___There are 7,000 students at his college.___

2. many majors / at the college _____

3. an instructor / for every course _____

4. 12 dorms / on the campus _____

5. elevators / in his dorm _____

6. a security guard / in his dorm _____

E Think about your bedroom or dorm room. Are the sentences true or false?
(Circle) the right answer.

1. There are two beds in the room.	True	False
2. There is a window next to my bed.	True	False
3. There is one pillow on my bed.	True	False
4. There is a dresser in the room.	True	False
5. There are three windows in the room.	True	False
6. There is a table next to my bed.	True	False
7. There is a computer in the room.	True	False
8. There are photographs in the room.	True	False

■ **C O M M U N I C A T E**

F WRITE Write about your school or college. Use *There is/There are* sentences.

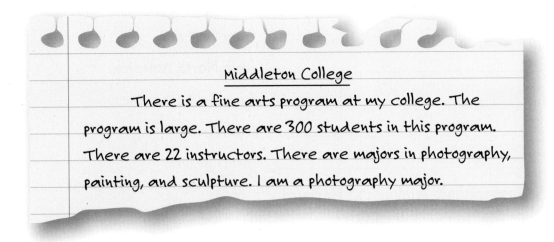

Middleton College
There is a fine arts program at my college. The
program is large. There are 300 students in this program.
There are 22 instructors. There are majors in photography,
painting, and sculpture. I am a photography major.

■ GRAMMAR IN CONTENT

TR10

A **Read and listen.**

The Right Program?

Receptionist:	This is the admissions office. Can I help you?
Marie:	Yes. I have a few questions. **Is there** a psychology program at the university?
Receptionist:	**Yes, there is.**
Marie:	**Are there** many international students in the program?
Receptionist:	**Yes, there are.** There are over 40 international students in the program.
Marie:	**Is there** a part-time program?
Receptionist:	**No, there isn't.**
Marie:	Oh, that's too bad. This isn't the right program for me.

admissions office: office in a school that helps people apply to the school

Is There/Are There Questions and Short Answers

Singular

Is + there	Subject	Location	Affirmative	Negative
Is there	a library	on campus?	Yes, there is.	No, there isn't.

Plural

Are + there	Subject	Location	Affirmative	Negative
Are there	students	in the classroom?	Yes, there are.	No, there aren't.

Notes:
- It is common to use *any* with *Are there* questions.
  Example: *Are there any night classes?*
- For negative answers, we usually use the contractions *isn't* and *aren't*.

B **Look at the dialogue "The Right Program?"** <u>Underline</u> **the questions with *Is there*** **and *Are there*.** (Circle) **the short answers.**

C Answer the questions. Use short answers.

Fast Facts about Parkhurst College

Programs		Yes	No
	Undergraduate	Yes	
	Graduate		No
	Part-time		No

Majors		Yes	No
	Mathematics		No
	Science	Yes	
	Social Sciences	Yes	
	Languages	Yes	
	Engineering		No
	Music		No
	Nursing	Yes	

Facilities		Yes	No
	Library	Yes	
	Academic Advising Office	Yes	
	Career Counseling Office	Yes	
	Computer Services	Yes	
	Student Parking		No
	Dorms		No

1. Is there a library at Parkhurst College? _____ *Yes, there is.* _____

2. Are there dorms at the college? _____

3. Are there graduate programs at the college? _____

4. Is there a mathematics program at the college? _____

5. Is there a music program at the college? _____

6. Is there a nursing program at the college? _____

7. Is there a Career Counseling Office at the college? _____

8. Are there part-time programs at the college? _____

D Complete the questions with *Is there* or *Are there*.

1. _____ *Is there* _____ an application form?

2. _____ a waiting list?

3. _____ graduate programs?

4. _____ a business program?

5. _____ students from South America?

6. _____ a part-time program?

7. _____ dorms on campus?

8. _____ computer labs on campus?

E PAIR WORK Ask and answer questions about your dorm, house, or apartment. Take turns.

Is there a washing machine in your dorm?

Yes, there is.

1. a closet?   2. vending machines?   3. an elevator?   4. parking spaces?

5. a telephone?   6. two beds?   7. a computer?   8. a washing machine?

F PAIR WORK Student A looks at the picture on this page. Student B looks at the picture on page 227. Find the differences. Ask and answer *Is there/Are there* questions. (Hint: There are six differences.)

Is there a blackboard in your picture?

Yes, there is.

GRAMMAR AND VOCABULARY Work with a partner. Partner A looks at the picture on this page. Partner B looks at the picture on page 227. Ask and answer questions to find out how your partner's picture is different from yours. How many differences can you find? Make notes on the differences. Use the grammar and vocabulary from this lesson.

Is there a music student in your picture?

Yes, there is. Actually, there are two music students in my picture.

PROJECT Create a pie chart about your classmates.
1. Work with your class.
2. Find out what countries your classmates are from.
3. Count how many students there are from each country.
4. Create a pie chart to show the results. Use the pie chart on page 35 as an example.
5. Make sentences about the results.

 INTERNET Go online. Search for a college or university that you are interested in. Find out how many students there are at this university. What programs does the university have? Report back to your class.

VOCABULARY JOURNAL Write sentences for new vocabulary you learned in this lesson.

Example: I am a <u>part-time</u> student. I only take classes two days a week.

B Read the sentences from the reading "The Busy Brain." (Circle) the correct word.

1. Jana (hear / (hears)) the alarm clock.
2. She (see / sees) the sun.
3. She (smell / smells) coffee.
4. The nerves (send / sends) information to the brain.
5. The brain (weigh / weighs) only about three pounds.

C Complete the sentences with the correct form of the verb in parentheses.

1. I (smell) _____smell_____ flowers.

4. I (hear) _____ birds.

2. He (smell) _____ hot dogs.

5. She (hear) _____ music.

3. They (smell) _____ garbage.

6. We (hear) _____ thunder.

D Correct the mistakes. Rewrite the sentences.

1. Every morning Ben bring Maria coffee.

   Every morning Ben brings Maria coffee.

2. She smell the coffee and wake up.

   _____

3. They makes breakfast.

   _____

4. Ben wash the dishes and Maria packs their lunches.

   _____

5. They leaves for work together.

   _____

■ **C O M M U N I C A T E**

E PAIR WORK Imagine you are in your favorite place. Complete the chart with information about it. Ask your partner about his or her favorite place and put the information in the chart. Tell the class about your favorite place and your partner's favorite place.

	Me	My Partner
1. What do you hear?		
2. What do you see?		
3. What do you smell?		
4. What do you taste?		
5. How do you feel?		

F WRITE Use the information in exercise E to write a paragraph about your favorite place and your partner's favorite place. Use the simple present tense.

PART TWO Spelling and Pronunciation of Third-Person *-s* Form

GRAMMAR IN CONTENT

Simple Present Spelling of Third-Person *-s* Form

Base Form	Spelling with *He, She,* or *It*	Rule
see	sees	Most verbs: Add -s
teach	teach**es**	Verbs that end in *sh, ch, x, z,* or *ss*: Add -es
study	stud**ies**	Verbs that end in consonant + *y*: Change *y* to *i* and add -es

A Circle the correct word.

1. Marco (studys / studies) biology.
2. He (takes / takies) classes all day.
3. At night he (works / workes) in the university.
4. He (hurryes / hurries) to the lab after classes.
5. He (cleanes / cleans) the laboratory.
6. He also (washs / washes) the equipment.
7. Marco (tries / trys) to study after work.
8. But he often (falles / falls) asleep.

B Write sentences about someone you know. Use the third-person form of the verb.

1. (live) ____________________
2. (watch) ____________________
3. (speak) ____________________
4. (study) ____________________
5. (eat) ____________________
6. (work) ____________________

The Simple Present Tense: Pronunciation of Verbs in the Third-Person -s Form	
Verbs That End In . . .	**Pronounce the Third-Person -s:**
the sounds *f, k, p,* or *t*	/s/ as in "eats"
the sounds *b, d, g, l, m, n, ng, r, v, y, a, e, i, o, u*	/z/ as in "lives"
ss, sh, ch, ce, se, ge, or *x*	/əz/ as in "teaches"

TR12

C Listen. Check (✔) the -s sound you hear.

		/s/ as in "eats"	/z/ as in "lives"	/əz/ as in "teaches"
1.			✔	
2.				
3.				
4.				
5.				
6.				
7.				
8.				
9.				
10.				

TR13

D Read each sentence aloud. Make sure you pronounce the third-person -s in the verb correctly. Then listen to the sentences to check your pronunciation.

1. Every day Jana **hears** her alarm clock.
2. She **sees** the sun.
3. She **feels** the water in the shower.
4. She **smells** coffee. She **tastes** her breakfast.
5. The brain **takes in** the information.
6. The brain **weighs** only about three pounds.

■ GRAMMAR IN CONTENT

A Read and listen.

TR14

Right Brain vs. Left Brain

The brain has two sides. Some scientists think right-brain and left-brain people **do not think** alike.

For example, Stacy loves numbers. She studies mathematics. She is organized. She **doesn't study** the arts. She is a left-brain person.

Tomek loves photography. He studies art. He **doesn't like** mathematics. He is creative. He is a right-brain person.

Stacy and Tomek **don't think** alike. But they are good friends.

alike: the same

organized: ordered, arranged

creative: having artistic skill or imagination

The Simple Present Tense: Negative Statements		
Subject	**Do Not (Don't)/ Does Not (Doesn't)**	**Base Verb**
I You We They	do not (don't)	study science.
He She It	does not (doesn't)	like photography.

Notes:

• The contraction for *do not* is *don't*.
• The contraction for *does not* is *doesn't*.

B Look at the reading "Right Brain vs. Left Brain." (Circle) the correct answer.

1. The brain ((has) / does not have) two sides.
2. Right-brain and left-brain people (think / do not think) alike.
3. Stacy (likes / doesn't like) numbers.
4. Tomek (likes / doesn't like) mathematics.
5. Stacy and Tomek (think / don't think) alike.

C Write negative sentences about yourself. Use the verbs provided and the simple present tense.

1. (study) _____
2. (live) _____
3. (need) _____
4. (enjoy) _____
5. (use) _____
6. (read) _____

D PAIR WORK Look at the sentences your partner wrote for exercise C. Make negative sentences about your partner.

1. (study) _____
2. (live) _____
3. (need) _____
4. (enjoy) _____
5. (use) _____
6. (read) _____

E **PAIR WORK** Find ten things that are different about you and your partner.

I speak Spanish.　　I don't speak Spanish.

F **WRITE** Write sentences about yourself and your partner. Share the list with your class.

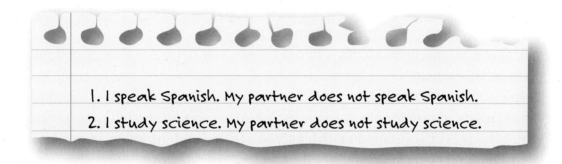

1. I speak Spanish. My partner does not speak Spanish.
2. I study science. My partner does not study science.

G **WRITE** Write a paragraph about things your partner does that you don't do. Use *but* to link the differences.

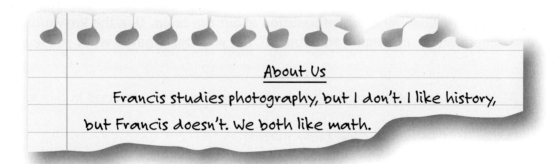

About Us
Francis studies photography, but I don't. I like history, but Francis doesn't. We both like math.

GRAMMAR AND VOCABULARY Work with a partner. Think of something you can see, hear, taste, or touch. Give your partner a clue about this thing. Keep giving more clues until your partner guesses the thing correctly. Use the grammar and vocabulary from this lesson.

You see this at the beach. There is a lot of it on the beach. It's brown. It's soft.

It's sand!

PROJECT Create a place.

1. Work with a group. Decide on a place together.
2. With your group, brainstorm a list of things you hear, see, feel, smell, and taste in this place.
3. Think of ways you can help your classmates hear, see, feel, smell, and taste these things. For example, for things you hear, you might make a recording or make the sound yourself. For things you see, you might bring in a photograph or draw a picture of things you might see at this place. Assign different students to prepare different things.
4. Set up your "place" in the classroom. Ask your classmates to say what they hear, see, feel, smell, and taste.
5. Ask your classmates to guess the place.

 INTERNET Go online. Look for more information about the brain. Use the keywords "brain" and "information" or "brain" and "facts." Tell your classmates what you learned.

VOCABULARY JOURNAL Write sentences for new vocabulary you learned in this lesson.

Example: *I hear my alarm clock every morning.*

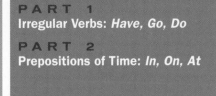
Health: Nursing

■ CONTENT VOCABULARY

Look at the pictures. Do you know the words?

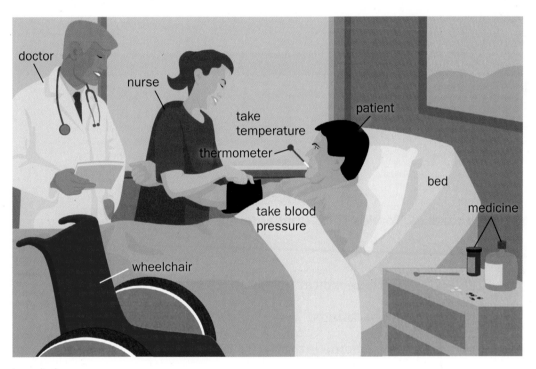

doctor

nurse

take temperature

thermometer

patient

bed

medicine

take blood pressure

wheelchair

hospital room

Write the new words in your vocabulary journal.

■ THINK ABOUT IT

Discuss these questions with a partner.

1. Where do nurses work?
2. What do nurses do?

■ GRAMMAR IN CONTENT

A Read and listen.

TR15

Mark's Job

Mark **has** a great job. He is a nurse. He works in a hospital. He **goes** to the hospital in the morning. He **does** many things. For example, he takes care of the patients. He takes their blood pressure and gives them medicine. He helps them into and out of wheelchairs. He helps the doctors. He often **goes** home late. He loves his job.

Irregular Verbs: *Have, Go, Do*	
I / You / We / They . . .	**He / She / It . . .**
. . . **have** a job.	. . . **has** a job.
. . . **go** to class every day.	. . . **goes** to class every day.
. . . **do** homework at the library.	. . . **does** homework at the library.

B Look at the reading "Mark's Job." Complete the sentences.

1. Mark _____has_____ a job.

2. He _____ to the hospital in the morning.

3. He _____ many things.

4. He often _____ home late.

C Read the sentences. If the sentence is correct, write "correct." If there is a problem, rewrite the sentence correctly.

1. Jake has a job in a hospital. _____ *correct* _____

2. Jenn have a job in an office. _____

3. She goes to work by car. _____

4. They has a lot of work to do. _____

5. Jake have lunch in the cafeteria. _____

6. They goes home at 5:00. _____

D Complete the sentences. Use the correct form of *have*, *go*, or *do*.

Aisha and Sabina are roommates. They live

together. They __*have*__ a nice apartment and
(1)

they _____ good jobs. They both work in St.
(2)

Mary's hospital. They _____ to work together
(3)

every morning.

Aisha is a doctor. She _____ many things
(4)

each day. She _____ many patients to take
(5)

care of. Sabina is a nurse. She _____ many things for the patients and the
(6)

doctors.

Sabina _____ home at about 5:00 every day. She _____ to the
(7)   (8)

supermarket after work. She cooks dinner. Aisha _____ home at about 7:00. They
(9)

_____ dinner together every night. Sabina cooks. Aisha _____ the dishes.
(10)   (11)

■ COMMUNICATE

E **WRITE** Write a paragraph about the job of someone you know. Use *have*, *go*, and *do* in the paragraph. Answer these questions:

- What job does the person have?
- Where does he or she go every day?
- What does he or she do?

Tell your class about the job.

■ GRAMMAR IN CONTENT

TR16

A Read and listen.

> **Just Relax!**
>
> John: You need to relax more.
>
> Linda: When? I take classes **in the morning**. I work at the hospital **in the afternoon**. I get home **at 6:00** every day. I do housework **in the evening**. I study **at night** and **on the weekend**. There is no time to relax!

relax: to stop working and enjoy oneself

Prepositions of Time: *In, On, At*	
Preposition	**Explanation**
in the morning **in** the afternoon **in** the evening **in** March **in** 2006	Use **in** with parts of the day and with months and years.
on Monday **on** weekends **on** January 3	Use **on** with days of the week, groups of days, and dates.
at 3:30 **at** night	Use **at** with times of day and with "night."

Note:
We often use "it" to talk about time, days, months, and years. Example: *It is April 8. It is 5:00.*

B Complete the sentences. Use *in, on,* or *at*.

1. John goes to school __*on*__ Monday, Wednesday, and Friday.

2. His classes are _____ the afternoon.

3. His first class starts _____ 1:00.

4. John has an appointment with his advisor _____ September 4.

5. The appointment is _____ the morning.

6. The appointment is _____ 9:00.

C Read Linda's schedule. Complete the sentences. Use *in*, *on*, or *at* and the correct information.

Schedule	Monday	Tuesday	Wednesday	Thursday	Friday
8:00–9:30	Anatomy	Biology	Anatomy	Biology	Anatomy
10:00–11:30	Study	Psychology	Study	Psychology	Study
12:00–12:30	Lunch	Lunch	Lunch	Lunch	Lunch
1:00–5:00	Work at the hospital	Work at the hospital	Work at the hospital	Work at the hospital	Work at the hospital

1. Linda's classes start __*at*__ __*8:00*__ every day.

2. She has biology class _____ _____ and _____.

3. She has anatomy class _____ _____, _____, and _____.

4. She eats lunch _____ _____ every day.

5. She finishes work _____ _____.

D Complete the sentences with information about yourself.

1. My birthday is in _____.

2. My birthday is on _____.

3. I get up at _____.

4. I have English class on _____.

5. My English class is at _____.

6. I get home at _____.

7. I _____ in the evening.

8. I _____ on the weekend.

■ **COMMUNICATE**

E **WRITE** Write your schedule for an average weekend. What do you do? Tell your class about your schedule.

Connection | Putting It Together

GRAMMAR AND VOCABULARY Choose one of the pictures. Write a paragraph about the picture. Make up information about the person's job and schedule. Use the grammar and vocabulary from this lesson.

paramedic

nurse

doctor

PROJECT Create and discuss a schedule.

1. Fill in the schedule with your own activities and appointments for this week.
2. Work with a partner. Imagine you want to study together this week.
3. Discuss your schedules and find a few times when you both can meet to study.

	Monday	Tuesday	Wednesday	Thursday	Friday	Saturday	Sunday
8:00 – 10:00							
10:00 – 12:00							
12:00 – 2:00							
2:00 – 4:00							
4:00 – 6:00							
6:00 – 8:00							

INTERNET Go online. Search for a hospital near where you live. Find information about the hospital. Tell your class about what you learned.

VOCABULARY JOURNAL Write sentences for new vocabulary you learned in this lesson.

Example: *Sick people take medicine.*

PART 1
The Simple Present Tense:
Yes/No Questions and Short Answers

PART 2
Simple Present *Wh-* Questions

Lesson 8

Media: Television

■ CONTENT VOCABULARY

Look at the pictures. Do you know these words?

reality show

sitcom

watch TV inside

news

sports

play outside

nature

game show

turn on/off

Write the new words in your vocabulary journal.

■ THINK ABOUT IT

Do you watch television? If so, do you watch:

___ less than one hour
a day?

___ one to two hours
a day?

___ more than two
hours a day?

■ GRAMMAR IN CONTENT

TR17

A **Read and listen.**

Interview with a Media Professor: Part 1

Interviewer:	**Do** American children **watch** a lot of television?
Dr. Teleno:	**Yes,** they **do**. Most of them watch three hours or more of TV a day.
Interviewer:	**Do** you **think** television is bad for children?
Dr. Teleno:	**Yes,** I **do**. Some programs are not good for children. Some children watch too much television. These children don't read enough. They also don't play outside enough.
Interviewer:	**Do** some programs **help** children learn?
Dr. Teleno:	**Yes,** they **do**. Some programs help children read.

enough: plenty, as much as needed

The Simple Present Tense: *Yes/No* Questions		
Do/Does	Subject	
Do	I you we they	watch TV?
Does	he she it	

Affirmative and Negative Short Answers					
Yes	Subject	*Do/Don't*	*No*	Subject	*Do/Don't*
Yes,	you I we they	do.	No,	you I we they	don't.
	he she it	does.		he she it	doesn't.

B Look at the dialogue "Interview with a Media Professor: Part 1." Answer the questions with short answers.

1. Do American children watch a lot of television? ____Yes, they do.____

2. Do they watch one hour of TV a day? _____

3. Do they watch three hours of TV a day? _____

4. Does Dr. Teleno think television is bad for children? _____

5. Do some programs help children learn? _____

C PAIR WORK Answer the questions about yourself. Use short answers. Then ask your partner the questions. Complete the chart with short answers.

	Me	My Partner
1. Do you like television?		
2. Do you watch the news?		
3. Do you watch sitcoms?		
4. Do you watch reality shows?		
5. Do you eat dinner with the television on?		
6. Do you study with the television on?		
7. Do you watch too much television?		

D Put the words in the correct order.

1. at night / you / do / watch television ____Do you watch television at night____?

2. no / don't / I _____, _____.

3. send e-mails / you / do / at night _____?

4. don't / no / I _____, _____.

5. study / do / at night / you _____?

6. I / do / yes _____, _____!

E Write *Yes/No* questions.

1. you / have / a television _____ *Do you have a television?* _____

2. you / rent / videos _____

3. you / watch / television in the evening _____

4. you / like / sitcoms _____

5. your wife / like / sports _____

6. she / control / the remote control _____

■ COMMUNICATE

F **GROUP WORK** What do your classmates do on the weekend? Ask your classmates *Yes/No* questions using the words in the chart. For each question, find a student who answers "Yes, I do." Write the student's name in the chart. Then report back to your class.

Do you . . .	Student's Name
 . . . watch TV?	
 . . . use the Internet?	
 . . . exercise at a gym?	
 . . . jog?	
 . . . garden?	
 . . . play an instrument?	

■ GRAMMAR IN CONTENT

TR18

 A **Read and listen.**

> **Interview with a Media Professor: Part 2**
>
> Interviewer: Do your children watch TV during the week?
> Dr. Teleno: No, they don't.
> Interviewer: **When do** they watch television?
> Dr. Teleno: They only watch television on weekends.
> Interviewer: **Why do** they watch TV only on weekends?
> Dr. Teleno: I want my children to do their homework and play outside.
> Interviewer: **What do** your children watch?
> Dr. Teleno: My daughter likes cartoons.
> Interviewer: **What does** your son like?
> Dr. Teleno: He likes nature programs.
> Interviewer: **Where do** they watch TV?
> Dr. Teleno: In the living room.

The Simple Present Tense: *Wh-* Questions

Wh- Word	*Do/Does*	Subject	Base Verb	Answers		
What	do	you	watch?	The news.	OR	I watch the news.
Where	does	she	live?	In California.	OR	She lives in California.
When	do	we	eat?	At 7:00.	OR	We eat at 7:00.
Who	does	he	love?	Marta.	OR	He loves Marta.
How	do	you	feel?	Good.	OR	I feel good.
Why	do	you	study?	(Because) I want good grades.		

Note:

When *Who* or *What* is the subject of a question, don't add *do* or *does* before the verb.

Example: *Who watches television?* (NOT: ~~Who does watch television?~~)

B **Look at the dialogue "Interview with a Media Professor: Part 2." Complete the questions. Then write answers to the questions.**

1. When __do__ Dr. Teleno's children watch TV? _____ *Only on weekends.* _____

2. Why _____ her children watch television only on weekends?

   _____

3. What _____ her children watch? _____

4. What _____ her son like? _____

5. Where _____ the children watch TV? _____

C Complete the questions. Write *wh-* words.

1. **Q:** _Who_ do you live with? **A:** I live with my husband and son.

2. **Q:** _____ do you study? **A:** I study computer science.

3. **Q:** _____ do you study computer science? **A:** Because I love computers.

4. **Q:** _____ do you relax? **A:** I watch television.

5. **Q:** _____ do you watch? **A:** I watch reality TV programs.

6. **Q:** _____ does your husband work? **A:** He works in an office.

7. **Q:** _____ does he relax? **A:** He reads the newspaper and watches the news.

8. **Q:** _____ does your son watch on TV? **A:** He watches cartoons.

D Complete the dialogue. Write *wh-* questions.

A: There's an interesting program on TV. It's about kangaroos.

B: Really? _Where do kangaroos live_ ?
(1)

A: Kangaroos live in Australia, Tasmania, and New Guinea.

B: _____ ?
(2)

A: They eat grass and leaves.

B: _____ ?
(3)

A: They eat in the late afternoon and early evening.

B: _____ during the day?
(4)

A: During the day they rest in the shade.

B: _____ get from one place to another?
(5)

A: They hop!

B: _____ communicate?
(6)

A: They thump their feet.

E PAIR WORK Write questions. Ask a partner each question. Write your partner's answers.

1. When / get up?

   Question: _____*When do you get up?*_____

   Answer: _____*Petra gets up at 7:00.*_____

2. What / eat for breakfast?

   Question: _____

   Answer: _____

3. Who / live with?

   Question: _____

   Answer: _____

4. How / get to school?

   Question: _____

   Answer: _____

5. What / do on weekends?

   Question: _____

   Answer: _____

6. When / study?

   Question: _____

   Answer: _____

■ COMMUNICATE

F PAIR WORK Ask your partner, "What do you do on the weekend?" Then interview your partner with *wh-* questions to find out more. Take notes.

What do you do on the weekend?

Where do you go shopping?

I study and go shopping.

GRAMMAR AND VOCABULARY Work with a partner. Ask your partner questions about his or her television habits. Use the grammar and vocabulary from this lesson.

> Do you like television?
>
> When do you watch television?

> Yes, I do.

PROJECT Create a bar graph about favorite TV shows.

1. With your class, discuss the following kinds of programs: reality shows, sitcoms, news, sports, nature shows, and game shows.
2. For each kind of show, take a vote: Who likes this kind of show best? Count the number of students who say it is their favorite.
3. Make a bar graph to show the results of your vote.

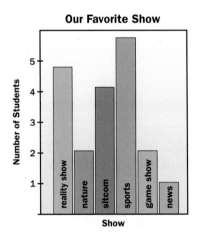

Our Favorite Show

 INTERNET Go online. Find out what is on television tonight. Use the keywords "television schedule." Imagine you will watch television tonight. Choose the programs you will watch.

VOCABULARY JOURNAL Write sentences for new vocabulary you learned in this lesson.

Example: *I think sitcoms are funny.*

PART 1
The Present Tense of *Be* vs.
the Simple Present Tense:
Statements

PART 2
The Present Tense of *Be* vs. the
Simple Present Tense: *Yes/No*
Questions and Short Answers

PART 3
The Present Tense of *Be* vs.
the Simple Present Tense:
Wh- Questions

Lesson 9

Biology: Studying Animals

■ CONTENT VOCABULARY

Look at the pictures. Do you know the words?

chimpanzee

elephant

nest

fruits

nuts

mice

leaves

insects

Write the new words in your vocabulary journal.

■ THINK ABOUT IT

Discuss these questions with a partner.

1. Do animals think?
2. What animal is most like people?

■ GRAMMAR IN CONTENT

A Read and listen.

TR19

Jane Goodall

Cynthia Moss

Two Famous Animal Researchers

Jane Goodall and Cynthia Moss **are** animal researchers. They **study** animals in Africa. Jane Goodall **studies** chimpanzees in Tanzania. Cynthia Moss **studies** elephants in Kenya.

Goodall and Moss **do** important work. Their work **helps** us understand chimpanzees and elephants.

researcher: person who studies something

The Present Tense of *Be* vs. the Simple Present Tense: Statements		
	Present Tense of *Be*	**Simple Present Tense**
Affirmative	I **am** a biology professor. He **is** a researcher.	I **teach** biology. He **studies** elephants.
Negative	I **am not** a researcher. He **is not** a biology professor.	I **do not study** elephants. He **does not teach** biology.

Note:
Don't use *be* with a simple present tense verb.
Example: *I study English.* (NOT: ~~I am study English.~~)

B Look at each sentence. Is the sentence the present tense of *be* or the simple present tense? (Circle) the correct answer.

1. Jane Goodall is an animal researcher. (Present Tense of *Be*)/ Simple Present Tense

2. Goodall and Moss study animals in Africa. Present Tense of *Be* / Simple Present Tense

3. She works with chimpanzees in Tanzania. Present Tense of *Be* / Simple Present Tense

4. Goodall and Moss do important work. Present Tense of *Be* / Simple Present Tense

C Read the sentences comparing two animal researchers. Fill in the blanks with the correct form of the underlined word(s).

1. I <u>study</u> chimpanzees. Dr. Ito _____studies_____ mice.

2. I <u>do not study</u> mice. Dr. Ito ___does not study___ chimpanzees.

3. He <u>works</u> with laboratory animals. I _____ with wild animals.

4. He <u>does not work</u> with wild animals. I _____ with laboratory animals.

5. I <u>am</u> from the United States. He _____ from Japan.

6. I <u>am not</u> from Japan. He_____ from the United States.

7. He <u>speaks</u> Japanese. I _____ English.

8. He <u>does not speak</u> English. I _____ Japanese.

9. I <u>am</u> married. He _____ single.

10. I <u>am not</u> single. He _____ married.

D Correct the composition. Cross out wrong words. Add missing words. (Hint: There are five more mistakes.)

<u>Elephants</u>

There are two kinds of elephants: African elephants and Indian elephants. Elephants ~~are~~ live for about 65 years. Elephants are not eat meat. They are eat 300 to 600 pounds of grass, leaves, and fruit each day. They drink 30 to 60 gallons of water each day.

Elephants lives in groups. Elephants are very intelligent. They are also very sensitive. They feels sad. They is cry. They even laugh!

■ COMMUNICATE

E WRITE Write a paragraph about an animal you know. What is the animal? What does it look like? What does it do? Use the present tense of *be* and the simple present tense. Tell your class about the animal.

PART TWO	The Present Tense of *Be* vs. the Simple Present Tense: *Yes/No* Questions and Short Answers

■ GRAMMAR IN CONTENT

TR20

A Read and listen.

Sue Savage Rumbaugh and Kanzi

Question:	Who is Sue Savage Rumbaugh?
Answer:	She's an animal researcher.
Question:	Who is Kanzi?
Answer:	Kanzi is a chimpanzee she works with.
Question:	**Is** he intelligent?
Answer:	Yes, he **is.**
Question:	**Does** Kanzi **understand** language?
Answer:	Yes, he **does.**
Question:	**Does** he **speak?**
Answer:	No, he **doesn't** speak.
Question:	How does he talk to people?
Answer:	He uses a special keyboard.
Question:	Why does she work with chimpanzees?
Answer:	Because chimpanzees and humans have similar brains.

keyboard: a row of keys

The Present Tense of *Be* vs. the Simple Present Tense: *Yes/No* Questions and Short Answers

	Yes/No Questions	Short Answers		
The Present Tense of Be	**Are** you a biology professor? **Is** he a biology professor?	Yes, I am. Yes, he **is.**	OR OR	No, I'm not. No, he **isn't.**
The Simple Present Tense	**Do** you **teach** biology? **Does** he **teach** biology?	Yes, I **do.** Yes, he **does.**	OR OR	No, I **don't.** No, he **doesn't.**

Note:
Don't use *be* with a simple present tense verb in a question.
Example: *Do you teach biology?* (NOT: ~~*Are you teach biology?*~~)

B Look again at the dialogue "Sue Savage Rumbaugh and Kanzi." Answer the questions. Use short answers.

1. Is Sue Savage Rumbaugh an animal researcher? _____ *Yes, she is.* _____

2. Is Kanzi an animal researcher? _____

3. Is Kanzi a chimpanzee? _____

4. Does he speak? _____

5. Does he understand language? _____

6. Do humans and chimpanzees have similar brains? _____

C Fill in the missing words in the questions and answers. Use *am, is, are, do, does, don't,* or *doesn't.*

1. _____ *Are* _____ you a biologist?   Yes, I _____ *am* _____.

2. _____ you work in a laboratory?   No, I _____.

3. _____ you study animals?   Yes, I _____.

4. _____ you study chimpanzees?   Yes, I _____.

5. _____ chimpanzees smart?   Yes, they _____.

6. _____ chimpanzees live alone?   No, they _____.

7. _____ they live in groups?   Yes, they _____.

8. _____ your work interesting?   Yes, it _____.

■ **C O M M U N I C A T E**

D **PAIR WORK** Choose an animal. Your partner will ask *Yes/No* questions to try to guess the animal. Take turns.

Does the animal live in North America?   Yes, it does.

Is it large?   No, it isn't.

Does it live in trees?   Yes, it does.

Is it a squirrel?   Yes, it is!

The Present Tense of *Be* vs. the Simple Present Tense: *Wh-* Questions

Wh- Questions with Present Tense of *Be*	*Wh-* Questions in the Simple Present Tense
Where is she? **Where are** they?	**Where does** she live? **Where do** they live?

Note:

Don't use *be* with a simple present tense verb in a question.

Example: *Where do they live?* (NOT: ~~Where are they live?~~)

A Look at the dialogue "Sue Savage Rumbaugh and Kanzi" on page 70. <u>Underline</u> the *wh-* questions with *be*. (Circle) the *wh-* questions in the simple present tense.

B Fill in the missing word in each question. Use *is, am, are, do,* or *does.*

1. **Q:** Where ____*do*____ chimpanzees live?

   A: Chimpanzees live in 21 African countries.

2. **Q:** What _____ the Afrikaans word for "chimpanzee"?

   A: Sjimpansee.

3. **Q:** What _____ chimpanzees eat?

   A: Fruits, nuts, leaves, insects, and sometimes meat.

4. **Q:** How _____ they communicate?

   A: With sounds and their bodies.

5. **Q:** Where _____ baby chimpanzees born?

   A: In a nest.

6. **Q:** How _____ a mother chimpanzee carry her baby?

   A: She carries the baby near her belly.

7. **Q:** How _____ a chimpanzee show love?

   A: Chimpanzees kiss and hug.

8. **Q:** How _____ chimpanzees and humans similar?

   A: The genes of chimpanzees and humans are 98% the same.

C Make questions for each statement.

1. **A:** My name is Svetlana.

   Q: What _____ *is your name* _____ ?

2. **A:** I speak Russian.

   Q: What language _____ ?

3. **A:** I am from Ukraine.

   Q: Where _____ ?

4. **A:** I get to school by bus.

   Q: How _____ ?

5. **A:** I study biology.

   Q: What _____ ?

6. **A:** I study biology because I love animals.

   Q: Why _____ ?

7. **A:** My favorite animals are elephants and tigers.

   Q: What _____ ?

8. **A:** Ms. Jacobs is my instructor.

   Q: Who _____ ?

■ COMMUNICATE

D **PAIR WORK** Create questions to ask your partner. Begin your questions with the words provided. Take turns asking questions. Tell the class what you learned about your partner.

1. What is . . . ?
2. Who is . . . ?
3. Where is . . . ?

4. Where do . . . ?
5. How do . . . ?
6. When do . . . ?
7. Why do . . . ?

E **WRITE** Imagine you are going to interview a zookeeper. What questions would you ask him/her? Write a list of your questions.

GRAMMAR AND VOCABULARY Ask and answer questions about the animals in this lesson. Use the grammar and vocabulary from this lesson.

What does a kangaroo eat?

Grass.

PROJECT Be an animal researcher.

1. Work in small groups.
2. Choose an animal you want to learn about.
3. Brainstorm a list of questions about this animal with your group.
4. Assign one or more questions to each student to research.
5. Research your question. Use the library and the Internet.
6. Report back to your group on what you learned.

 INTERNET Go online. Search for more information on the work of Jane Goodall, Cynthia Moss, or Sue Savage Rumbaugh. Tell your class about what you found out.

VOCABULARY JOURNAL Write sentences for new vocabulary you learned in this lesson.

Example: <u>Birds</u> keep eggs in their nests.

PART 1
Adverbs of Frequency

PART 2
Questions with *How Often;*
Frequency Expressions

Lesson 10

Health: Stress

■ CONTENT VOCABULARY

Look at the pictures. Do you know the words?

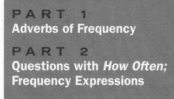

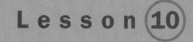

worried   in a rush   headache   stomachache

relax   exercise   sleep   go out with friends

Write the new words in your vocabulary journal.

■ THINK ABOUT IT

Discuss these questions with a partner.

1. What things make people feel stress?
2. What helps people relax?

■ GRAMMAR IN CONTENT

A **Read and listen.**

TR21

Stress

John is a computer science student. He **often** feels stress. He and his wife wake up at 6:30. They get their children ready for school. Then he takes the train to school. He **usually** studies on the train. He is **often** late for class. He goes to school all day and works in the evening. He **usually** gets home after 8:00. He **rarely** relaxes. He **rarely** sleeps well.

Stress is a problem for many people. It **sometimes** causes medical problems. It affects the heart and brain in many ways.

ready: prepared

cause: to make something happen

affect: to change

Adverbs of Frequency		
Frequency Words	**Examples with *Be***	**Examples with the Simple Present Tense**
100% **Always**	He is **always** late.	I **always** study in the library.
Usually	You are **usually** early.	He **usually** wakes up at 7:00.
Often	They are **often** busy.	She **often** works late.
Sometimes	We are **sometimes** in a rush.	They **sometimes** relax at home.
Rarely	My mother is **rarely** angry.	I **rarely** exercise.
0% **Never**	I am **never** wrong.	The shop is **never** closed.

Notes:
- Use adverbs of frequency to say how often something happens.
- Put adverbs of frequency after the verb *be*. Example: *I am **always** early.*
- Put adverbs of frequency before all other verbs. Example: *She **usually** works late.*

B Look at the reading "Stress." Compare yourself to John. Use the frequency words that are true for you.

1. John **often** feels stress.   I _____ feel stress.

2. He is **often** late for class.   I am _____ late for class.

3. He **usually** gets home after 8:00.   I _____ get home after 8:00.

4. He **rarely** relaxes.   I _____ relax.

5. He **rarely** sleeps well.   I _____ sleep well.

C Rewrite each sentence. Put the adverb of frequency in the right place.

1. Zoya is late for class. (usually) _____ *Zoya is usually late for class.* _____

2. She is on time. (rarely) _____

3. She is tired in the morning. (always) _____

4. Karl is on time. (usually) _____

5. He is late. (rarely) _____

6. He is tired in the morning. (never) _____

D Rewrite each sentence. Put the adverb of frequency in the right place.

1. Zoya studies at night. (always) _____ *Zoya always studies at night.* _____

2. She watches television. (sometimes) _____

3. She goes to bed late. (usually) _____

4. She hears the alarm clock. (rarely) _____

5. She gets up late. (often) _____

6. She misses her bus. (often) _____

E Take this stress test. Choose the adverbs of frequency that are true for you. Then add up the number of each of your answers to find your score.

The Stress Test

1. I _____ feel nervous.
　　1—always　　2—usually　　3—sometimes　　4—rarely　　5—never

2. I _____ feel worried.
　　1—always　　2—usually　　3—sometimes　　4—rarely　　5—never

3. I am _____ in a rush.
　　1—always　　2—usually　　3—sometimes　　4—rarely　　5—never

4. People _____ tell me to relax.
　　1—always　　2—usually　　3—sometimes　　4—rarely　　5—never

5. I _____ get headaches.
　　1—always　　2—usually　　3—sometimes　　4—rarely　　5—never

6. I _____ have stomachaches.
　　1—always　　2—usually　　3—sometimes　　4—rarely　　5—never

7. I _____ have sleep problems.
　　1—always　　2—usually　　3—sometimes　　4—rarely　　5—never

8. I am _____ sad.
　　1—always　　2—usually　　3—sometimes　　4—rarely　　5—never

8–16　There is a lot of stress in your life.
17–24　There is an average amount of stress in your life.
25–40　There is very little stress in your life.

■ **C O M M U N I C A T E**

F **WRITE** Describe a typical day for you. Use each adverb of frequency at least once. Tell your class about your typical day.

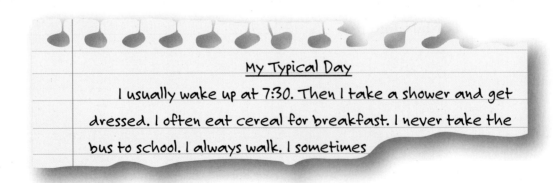

My Typical Day

I usually wake up at 7:30. Then I take a shower and get dressed. I often eat cereal for breakfast. I never take the bus to school. I always walk. I sometimes

■ GRAMMAR IN CONTENT

TR22

A **Read and listen.**

Doctor's Orders

Patient: I feel stress all the time.

Doctor: You need to take care of yourself. **How often** do you get eight hours of sleep?

Patient: **Every day.**

Doctor: Great. **How often** do you eat a well-balanced meal?

Patient: Maybe **once or twice a week.**

Doctor: You must eat healthy meals **three times a day. How often** do you exercise?

Patient: **Three or four times a month.**

Doctor: That's not good. Your body needs exercise **every day.** And you must relax more.

Patient: You're right doctor. I need to change my habits.

well balanced: healthy combination

Questions with *How Often*
How often do you go to the doctor?
How often do you exercise?
How often do you go out with friends?

Frequency Expressions	
once	
twice	a day / a week / a month / a year
three times	
every day, every night, every week, every month	

Note:

You can answer *How often* questions with just a frequency expression or with a full sentence that has a frequency expression. Example:

Q: How often do you go to the doctor?
A: Once a year.   OR   *I go to the doctor once a year.*

B Look again at the dialogue "Doctor's Orders." Answer the questions.

1. How often does the patient get eight hours of sleep? _____ *every day* _____

2. How often does she eat a well-balanced meal? _____

3. How often does the doctor want her to eat a healthy meal? _____

_____

4. How often does she exercise? _____

5. How often does the doctor want her to exercise? _____

C Answer the questions. Compare your answers with a partner.

1. How often do you get eight hours of sleep? _____

2. How often do you exercise? _____

3. How often do you eat vegetables? _____

4. How often do you drink coffee or tea? _____

5. How often do you go out with friends? _____

D Listen to the woman talk about her schedule. (Circle) the correct answers.

TR23

1. How often does she clean the house?
   a. once a week (b. twice a week) c. every day

2. How often does she do the laundry?
   a. every day b. once a week c. four times a week

3. How often does she cook dinner?
   a. every day b. every week c. every month

4. How often does she take her kids to soccer practice?
   a. once a week b. twice a week c. three times a week

5. How often does she drink a cup of coffee?
   a. once a day b. three times a day c. six times a day

6. How often does she have trouble sleeping?
   a. every night b. once a week c. twice a week

PART 1
The Present Progressive Tense:
Affirmative

PART 2
Spelling of Verbs in the *-ing* Form

PART 3
The Present Progressive Tense:
Negative

Education: Learning Styles

■ CONTENT VOCABULARY

Look at the pictures. Do you know the words?

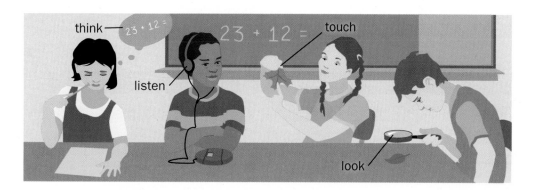

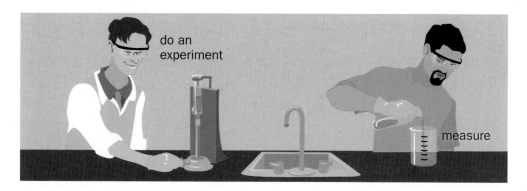

Write the new words in your vocabulary journal.

■ THINK ABOUT IT

Check (✔) what you are doing right now.

I am . . .

reading. ___   listening to something. ___

thinking. ___   looking at something. ___

■ GRAMMAR IN CONTENT

TR24

A **Read and listen.**

Learning Styles

I'm an elementary school teacher. I **am teaching** a first grade class right now. The children **are learning** about autumn. Different students **are learning** in different ways. Bina learns best with her eyes. She **is looking** at pictures of autumn. Michael learns well with his ears. He's **listening** to a story about autumn. Anna learns best with her hands. She's **touching** leaves. Researchers call these different ways of learning "learning styles."

autumn: the season between summer and winter (also called **fall**)

The Present Progressive Tense: Affirmative			
Subject	*Be*	**Verb + -ing**	**Contraction**
I	am	thinking.	I'm thinking.
He She It	is	learning.	He's learning.
You We They	are	listening to music.	They're listening to music.

Notes:

- Use the present progressive to talk about something happening (or not happening) right now.
- To form the present progressive tense of a verb, add *-ing* to the end of most verbs. For verbs with special spellings in the present progressive, see Part Two of this lesson.
- Use "It" with the present progressive to talk about weather. Example: *It is raining.*

B **Look at the reading "Learning Styles."** (Circle) **the correct form of the verb.**

1. The teacher (is teach / (is teaching)) a class.
2. The students (is learning / are learning) about autumn.
3. Bina (looks / is looking) at a book.
4. Michael (am listening to / is listening to) a story.
5. Anna (are touching / is touching) leaves.

C **What is happening right now? Check (✔) the true sentences.**

1. My instructor is talking. ___
2. The students are listening. ___
3. I am standing. ___
4. I am holding a pen. ___

5. A student is drinking water. ___
6. Some students are reading. ___
7. It is raining outside. ___
8. I am thinking about lunch. ___

D **Complete the paragraph. Use the present progressive affirmative of the verbs.**

Right now, Mr. Hudson (teach) ___*is teaching*___ the class. I

(listen) _____(2)_____ to Mr. Hudson's lecture. It's very interesting.

The other students (think) _____(3)_____ about the lesson.

Zara (ask) _____(4)_____ a question. Mr. Hudson

(write) _____(5)_____ the answer on the board. Two students

(talk) _____(6)_____.

E **Write present progressive sentences with the words provided.**

Tomoko and Bill learn best with their eyes.

1. Tomoko / look at / a chart
   _____*Tomoko is looking at a chart.*_____

Tomoko   Bill

2. Bill / watch / a DVD _____

Carlo and Claudia learn best with their ears.

3. Carlo / listen to / a CD

   _____

Carlo   Claudia

4. Claudia / listen to / a lecture _____

Jenn and Yakov learn best with their hands.

5. Jenn / do / an experiment

   _____

Jenn   Yakov

6. Yakov / touch / a rock _____

F Correct the student paragraph. There are eight more mistakes.

What's Happening?

My name is Alicia. Right now I ~~am~~ sitting in Introduction to Education class. I am learn about elementary education. The teacher talk about second grade students. Cara and Ben listening. Amir's cell phone is ring. Outside, a few students playing soccer. Sarah is look out the window and watch them.

■ COMMUNICATE

G **GROUP WORK** Work in groups of four. One student pretends to do something. The other students guess what the student is doing. Take turns.

You're taking a photo!

That's right.

PART TWO	Spelling of Verbs in the *-ing* Form

Spelling of Verbs in the *-ing* Form

Base Form	*-ing* Form	Rules:
work eat	working eating	For most verbs: Add *-ing*.
live write	living writing	For verbs that end in a consonant + *e*: Drop the *e* and add *-ing*. Do not double the consonant. Wrong: ~~writting~~
sit plan	sitting planning	For one-syllable verbs that end in *one* vowel + one consonant: Double the consonant and add *-ing*.
say sleep listen think	saying sleeping listening thinking	Do not double the last consonant before *-ing* when the verb: • ends in *w, x,* or *y*. • ends in two vowels and then one consonant. • has more than one syllable (when the stress is on the first syllable). • ends in two or more consonants.

A Write the *-ing* form of the verbs.

1. take _____taking_____ 4. stop _____ 7. sit _____

2. read _____ 5. ride _____ 8. use _____

3. smile _____ 6. write _____ 9. sleep _____

B Look at the picture of the school yard. Complete the sentences with the present progressive form of one of the verbs in the box. Use the correct spelling.

| eat | run | sit | write | read | ~~smile~~ | ride | drink |

1. The teacher _____is smiling_____.

2. Bianca _____ a sandwich.

3. Darell _____ milk.

4. Duong _____.

5. Lilly _____ in her notebook.

6. Pedro and Jack _____ bicycles.

7. Mikey and Lily _____ on the ground.

8. Mikey _____ a book.

■ COMMUNICATE

C **GROUP WORK** The class forms two teams. Team A says a verb. Someone from Team B writes the progressive form of the verb on the board. The first team to spell ten words correctly wins.

■ GRAMMAR IN CONTENT

TR25

A Read and listen.

Learning by Doing

Ming-Shan is learning about math. He **is not sitting** in math class. He **is not listening** to a teacher. He**'s not doing** homework. How is he learning about math? Ming-Shan is measuring sugar. He's helping his mother bake a cake.

bake: to cook something in an oven, for example bread or cakes

Present Progressive Negative Statements with *Be*; Negative Contractions with *Be*					
Subject	***Be* + Not**	**Verb + *-ing***	**Contraction**		
I	am not	sleeping.	I'm not sleeping.		
He			He **isn't** working.	OR	He**'s not** working.
She	is not	working.	She **isn't** working.	OR	She**'s not** working.
It			It **isn't** working.	OR	It**'s not** working.
You			You **aren't** listening.	OR	You**'re not** listening.
We	are not	listening.	We **aren't** listening.	OR	We**'re not** listening.
They			They **aren't** listening.	OR	They**'re not** listening.

B Look at these sentences about the reading "Learning by Doing." (Circle) true or false.

1. Ming-Shan is learning about math.   True   False
2. He's not doing homework.   True   False
3. He is listening to a teacher.   True   False
4. He's not helping his mother bake a cake.   True   False
5. Ming-Shan is measuring sugar.   True   False
6. He is sitting in a classroom.   True   False

C Write *true* or *false*. If false, write a negative sentence.

1. I am drinking coffee. _____ *False. I am not drinking coffee.*

2. I am learning grammar. _____

3. It is raining. _____

4. I am doing an exercise. _____

5. My instructor is writing on the board. _____

6. My instructor is sleeping. _____

7. The person in front of me is reading a newspaper.

    _____

8. The person behind me is talking. _____

■ C O M M U N I C A T E

D **PAIR WORK** Student A looks at the picture on this page. Student B looks at the picture on page 227. Talk about your pictures. Find the five differences. Use the present progressive.

John is reading in my picture.

He isn't reading in my picture.

GRAMMAR AND VOCABULARY Look around your classroom. Write a paragraph about what you, your instructor, and your classmates are doing or not doing. Use the grammar and vocabulary from the lesson. Read your paragraph to the class.

PROJECT Create a photo collage of school activities.

1. Work in groups of three students.
2. Find or take photos of people doing things at school.
3. Create a collage of these activities.
4. What are the people doing in the pictures? Label each activity.
5. Show your collage to the class.

INTERNET Go online. Find news stories with photographs. Use the key word "news." What is happening in the photographs? Tell your classmates.

VOCABULARY JOURNAL Write sentences for new vocabulary you learned in this lesson.

Example: I am thinking about my homework.

PART 1
The Present Progressive Tense:
Yes/No Questions and Short
Answers

PART 2
The Present Progressive Tense:
Wh- Questions

Lesson 12

Computer Science: Computer Literacy

■ CONTENT VOCABULARY

Look at the pictures. Do you know the words?

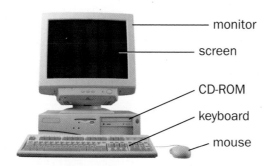

monitor

screen

CD-ROM

keyboard

mouse

desktop computer

laptop computer

Internet

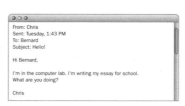

From: Chris
Sent: Tuesday, 1:43 PM
To: Bernard
Subject: Hello!

Hi Bernard,

I'm in the computer lab. I'm writing my essay for school.
What are you doing?

Chris

e-mail

printer

Write the new words in your vocabulary journal.

■ THINK ABOUT IT

Check (✔) what you can use a computer to do.

I can use a computer to . . .

write papers. ___   do research. ___   play music. ___

send e-mail. ___   play computer games. ___   (what else?). _____

GRAMMAR IN CONTENT

A Read and listen.

TR26

In the Computer Lab

Lab assistant:	**Is** this computer **working?**
Student:	Yes, it **is.**
Lab assistant:	**Are** you **using** it?
Student:	Yes, I **am.**
Lab assistant:	**Are** you **doing** research?
Student:	No, I**'m** not.
Lab assistant:	**Are** you **writing** a paper?
Student:	No, I**'m** not. I**'m** playing a computer game.
Lab assistant:	Sorry. No computer games in the lab.
Student:	Oh, OK. I**'m** sorry!

The Present Progressive Tense:
Yes/No Questions

Be	Subject	Verb + -ing
Am	I	standing?
Is	he she it	working?
Are	you we they	writing?

Short Answers

	Affirmative				Negative	
Yes	**Subject**	**Be**		**No**	**Subject + Be + Not**	
Yes,	I	am.		No,	I'm not.	
	he she it	is.			he **isn't.** OR he**'s not.** she **isn't.** OR she**'s not.** it **isn't.** OR it**'s not.**	
	you we they	are.			you **aren't.** OR you**'re not.** we **aren't.** OR we**'re not.** they **aren't.** OR they**'re not.**	

B Look at the dialogue "In the Computer Lab." Give a short answer for each question.

1. Is the computer working? _____ *Yes, it is.* _____

2. Is the student using it? _____

3. Is he doing research? _____

4. Is he writing a paper? _____

5. Is he playing a computer game? _____

C Look at the picture. Write *yes/no* questions and short answers about it.

1. (Ivanna / stand next to the printer)

   Q: ___Is Ivanna standing next to the printer___ ?   A: _____Yes, she is_____.

2. (Elena and Hanif / use laptops)

   Q: _____?   A: _____.

3. (Hanif / sit between Elena and Ivanna)

   Q: _____?   A: _____.

4. (Tan / putting a CD-ROM in the computer)

   Q: _____?   A: _____.

5. (Ivanna and Tan / wear blue shirts)

   Q: _____?   A: _____.

6. (Elena / using the mouse)

   Q: _____?   A: _____.

■ **COMMUNICATE**

D **PAIR WORK** Ask and answer present progressive questions with a partner. Use the words provided. Then make up more present progressive questions to ask your partner. Take turns.

Are we practicing the present progressive?   Yes, we are.

1. we / practice the present progressive
2. we / practice the past tense
3. I / sit next to a window
4. you / wear jeans
5. the instructor / write on the board
6. the instructor / explain the grammar

E **GROUP WORK** Work in groups of three students. One student thinks of a person in class. The others ask questions to guess the person. Take turns.

Is she wearing a red shirt and blue jeans?

Is she writing in her notebook?

Yes, she is.

No, she isn't.

PART TWO	The Present Progressive Tense: *Wh-* Questions

■ GRAMMAR IN CONTENT

TR27

A Read and listen.

Writing an E-mail

Mai:	**What are** you **doing?**
Keiko:	I'm writing an e-mail.
Mai:	**Who are** you **writing** to?
Keiko:	I'm writing to Inez.
Mai:	**Why are** you **writing** to Inez?
Keiko:	We're making plans to get together.
Mai:	You aren't typing anymore. What's wrong?
Keiko:	You're asking too many questions. It's hard to concentrate.

concentrate: to focus, to think hard about something

The Present Progressive Tense: *Wh-* Questions

Wh- Word	*Be*	Subject	Verb + *-ing*	Answers		
Who	am	I	**talking** to?	Eduardo.	OR	You're talking to Eduardo.
What	are	you	**doing?**	Writing.	OR	I'm writing an e-mail.
Where	is	Lola	**studying?**	The lab.	OR	She's studying in the lab.
How	are	you	**feeling?**	Fine.	OR	I'm feeling fine.
Why	is	she	**crying?**	Because she's sad.		

Note:

The question "What . . . doing?" is often answered with a different verb.

Example: *What are you **doing?** I'm **writing** a letter.*

C Complete the paragraph. Use the simple present or the present progressive form of the verbs in parentheses.

Right now I (write) _____am writing_____ in my journal. It (rain)
(1)

_____ outside. I (think) _____ about my family. I often
(2)   (3)

(think) _____ about my family. I am in LA. My family is in Japan.
(4)

I (speak) _____ with my family every weekend. My mother (send)
(5)

_____ me letters every week. But I still miss them. Oh! The phone
(6)

(ring) _____. Maybe my father (call) _____. He always
(7)   (8)

(call) _____ on Sunday.
(9)

D Complete the sentences with a negative statement.

1. Raj is studying in the library now. Tanya _is not studying in the library now_.

2. Tanya is writing in her journal now. Raj _____.

3. Raj is using a dictionary now. Tanya _____.

4. Tanya writes poems in her journal. Raj _____.

5. Raj draws pictures in his journal. Tanya _____.

6. Raj shows Tanya his journal. Tanya _____.

E Correct the journal entry. There are six more mistakes.

Thursday, July 23

                                              eating
I usually eat lunch in the cafeteria. Today I'm eat lunch outside. The
                                              ^

sun shining. It's a beautiful day. I'm watching people around me, and I'm

writing in my journal. Many people is sitting in the sun. I usually don't

sitting in the sun. I sit in the shade. And I wears sunscreen. Some people

are playing ball. A man are playing a guitar. Everyone is having fun! I

usually studying in the library after lunch. But not today.

F **WRITE** Write a journal entry. Write about the things happening around you. What are you doing? What are your classmates doing?

G **WRITE** Write a journal entry about activities you do often. Tell about any hobbies and interests you have. Do any of your friends or family members have similar hobbies or interests?

PART TWO	The Simple Present Tense vs. the Present Progressive Tense: *Yes/No* Questions

■ GRAMMAR IN CONTENT

TR29

A **Read and listen.**

Interview with an English Instructor

Interviewer:	**Do** your students **write** in journals?
Professor Harris:	Yes, they **do.**
Interviewer:	**Are** they **writing** in their journals now?
Professor Harris:	Yes, they **are.**
Interviewer:	**Are** they **writing** about themselves?
Professor Harris:	Yes, they **are.** They're writing about their feelings, ideas, problems, and memories.
Interviewer:	**Do** your students **worry** about spelling and punctuation in their journals?
Professor Harris:	No, they **don't.**
Interviewer:	**Do** they **write** in their journals every day?
Professor Harris:	Yes, they **do.**

The Simple Present Tense vs. the Present Progressive Tense: *Yes/No* Questions

	Yes/No Questions	Short Answers
Simple Present	**Do** you **teach** an English class? **Does** she **teach** an English class?	Yes, I **do.** OR No, I **don't.** Yes, she **does.** OR No, she **doesn't.**
Present Progressive	**Are** you **teaching** an English class now? **Is** she **teaching** an English class now?	Yes, I **am.** OR No, I'm **not.** Yes, she **is.** OR No, she **isn't.**

B Look at the dialogue "Interview with an English Instructor." Answer the questions with short answers.

1. Do Professor Harris's students keep journals? _____ *Yes, they do.* _____

2. Are they writing in their journals now? _____

3. Are they writing about themselves? _____

4. Do they worry about spelling in their journals? _____

5. Do they write in their journals every day? _____

C Listen to each question. (Circle) the correct answer.

TR30

1. (a.) Yes, she does.   b. Yes, she is.
2. a. No, she doesn't.   b. No, she isn't.
3. a. Yes, they do.   b. Yes, they are.
4. a. No, they don't.   b. No, they aren't.
5. a. Yes, you do.   b. Yes, you are.
6. a. Yes, you do.   b. Yes, you are.

D Write questions for the answers.

1. _*Is Amy sitting in the right chair?*_ Yes, Amy is sitting in the right chair.

2. _____ Yes, she always sits in that chair.

3. _____ Yes, we are listening to the instructor.

4. _____ Yes, we always listen to the instructor.

5. _____ Yes, I am writing in my journal now.

6. _____ No, I don't write in my journal every day.

E Rewrite the questions correctly.

1. Is it rain now? _____ *Is it raining now?* _____

2. Is it rain every day? _____

3. Does she using a computer every day?

_____

4. She using a computer now? _____

5. Does you often use a dictionary? _____

6. You use a dictionary right now? _____

Part Two | The Simple Present Tense vs. the Present Progressive Tense: *Yes/No* Questions   **103**

F **PAIR WORK** Ask your partner a simple present tense *yes/no* question with a phrase in the box. Then ask your partner a present progressive *yes/no* question with the same phrase. Take turns. Ask more questions using your own phrases.

read the newspaper	watch TV	speak English	write in a journal
think about grammar	wear jeans	drink coffee	use a dictionary

Do you read the newspaper every day?

Are you reading the newspaper now?

Yes, I do.

No, I'm not.

PART THREE	The Simple Present Tense vs. the Present Progressive Tense: *Wh-* Questions

■ GRAMMAR IN CONTENT

TR31

A **Read and listen.**

Starting a Journal

Student: I want to start a journal, but I have so many questions. What **do** journal writers **write** about? When **do** they **write**? How **do** they **start**?

Professor Harris: It's simple. Think about these questions: How **are** you **feeling** right now? What **are you doing**? What **are** you **thinking** about? Look around you. Who **do** you **see**? What **are** people **doing**? Now get a pen and paper and write.

simple: not complicated

The Simple Present Tense vs. the Present Progressive Tense: *Wh-* Questions	
Simple Present	**Present Progressive**
What do you **write** about in your journal?	**What are** you **writing** about in your journal?
What languages **does she speak**?	**What** language **is** she **speaking** now?
Where do they **work**?	**Where are** they **working** today?
Where does he **go** after school?	**Where is** he **going** now?

B Look at each question. Is it the simple present or the present progressive tense? (Circle) the correct answer.

1. What do journal writers write about? (Simple Present) / Present Progressive
2. What are you doing? Simple Present / Present Progressive
3. When do they write? Simple Present / Present Progressive
4. What do you see? Simple Present / Present Progressive
5. What are you thinking about? Simple Present / Present Progressive

C (Circle) the correct question.

1. (a.) What does John study? b. What does John studying?
2. a. What language do you speak? b. What language are you speak?
3. a. Where am I go? b. Where am I going?
4. a. Where are you going now? b. Where do you going now?
5. a. Why are they smiling? b. Why does they smiling?
6. a. What are we doing? b. What do we doing?
7. a. Who does you writing about? b. Who are you writing about?

D Write the correct form of the verb in parentheses.

A: Who are you (write) ___writing___ about?
(1)

B: My mother. She's a nurse.

A: Where does she (work) _____ ?
(2)

B: She (work) _____ at Brookville Hospital.
(3)

A: What is she (do) _____ now?
(4)

B: She's (sleep) _____ .
(5)

A: Why is she (sleep) _____ ?
(6)

B: She (come) _____ home from the hospital very late.
(7)

■ **COMMUNICATE**

E **GROUP WORK** Think about a friend or family member. What is his/her name? Where is he/she? What is he/she doing right now? Ask your classmates about their friends or family members. Complete the chart.

Name of Friend	Location of Friend	What Friend Is Doing

GRAMMAR AND VOCABULARY Write a letter or e-mail to someone you know. Use the grammar and vocabulary from this lesson.

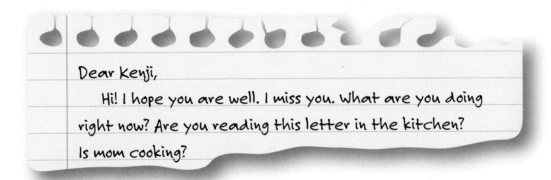

> Dear Kenji,
>
> Hi! I hope you are well. I miss you. What are you doing right now? Are you reading this letter in the kitchen? Is mom cooking?

PROJECT Start a writing journal.

1. Buy a notebook.
2. Each day write a journal entry in your notebook. Start each entry with the date. Then write about your thoughts, feelings, and problems.
3. Keep writing in your journal until the end of the course.
4. At the end of the course, read your journal.

 INTERNET Go online. Search the news headlines and report back to the class on what's happening today. Do these things happen often? Discuss.

VOCABULARY JOURNAL Write sentences for new vocabulary you learned in this lesson.

Example: *I wrote a poem for my boyfriend on Valentine's Day.*

Sociology: The Family

■ CONTENT VOCABULARY

Look at Sarah's family tree. Do you know the words?

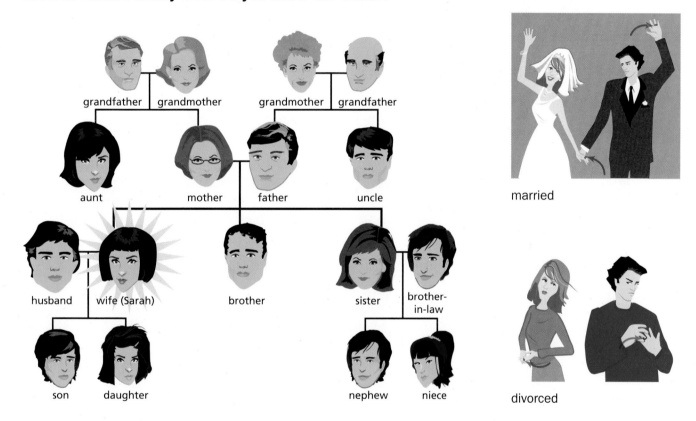

grandfather   grandmother   grandmother   grandfather

aunt   mother   father   uncle

married

husband   wife (Sarah)   brother   sister   brother-in-law

son   daughter   nephew   niece

divorced

Write the new words in your vocabulary journal.

■ THINK ABOUT IT

Discuss these questions with a partner.

1. Who are the people in your family?
2. Why are families important?

■ GRAMMAR IN CONTENT

TR32

A Read and listen.

One Family

What is a family? A traditional family is a mother, a father, and their children. But families are often more complicated. For example, **Jenn's** parents are divorced. Jenn lives with her mother, her stepfather, and her **stepfather's** daughter.

Jenn's last name is Maslin. This is her **father's** last name. Her **mother's** last name is Roberts. This is her **mother's** maiden name. And her **stepfather's** and **stepsister's** last name is Brown.

traditional: usual, customary

maiden name: a woman's family name before she marries

stepfather: father by marriage

Possessive Nouns

Nouns	Explanation	Examples
Singular nouns: Karen, brother	add apostrophe (') + s	**Karen's** house is small. Her **brother's** wife is nice.
Plural nouns that end in -s: sons, dogs	add apostrophe (') only	My **sons'** names are Dan and John. The **dogs'** dishes are empty.
Irregular plural nouns: women, children	add apostrophe (') + s	The **women's** room is to the left. The **children's** toys are on the floor.

B Complete the sentences with the possessive form of the nouns in parentheses.

1. (Mark) _____*Mark's*_____ parents are divorced.

2. Their (mother) _____ name is Maria.

3. My (parent) _____ house is large.

4. The (children) _____ school is across the street.

5. Diane is a (woman) _____ name.

6. Diane and Karen are (women) _____ names.

C Look at the family tree. Complete the sentences about Ben and his family. Use possessive nouns.

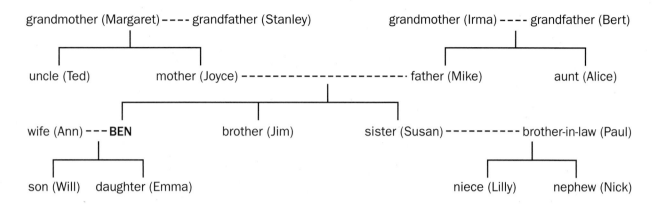

1. Ben is married. His _____wife's_____ name is Ann.

2. His _____ name is Will.

3. Joyce is his _____ name.

4. Bert is his _____ name.

5. Will and Emma are his _____ names.

6. Stanley is _____Margaret's_____ husband.

7. Nick is _____ brother.

8. Lilly is _____ sister.

9. Lilly is _____ niece.

D PAIR WORK Work with a partner to make more sentences about the family tree in exercise C.

■ COMMUNICATE

E PAIR WORK Draw a family tree for your family. Then use your family tree to tell your partner about your family.

■ GRAMMAR IN CONTENT

A Read and listen.

TR33

A Family from Mexico

Amato is part of a Mexican family. His family is very close. He lives with **his** mother, father, and sister. Amato's sister is seven years old. **Her** name is Marta. **Their** father is the head of the house. **His** name is Cristo. **Their** mother is the heart of the family. **Her** name is Isabel. **Their** grandmother and grandfather also live with them. **Their** aunts, uncles, and cousins live nearby.

close: not far apart, near

head of the house: the leader of the family

nearby: close by

Possessive Adjectives		
Subject Pronoun	Possessive Adjective	Example
I	my	**My** name is Emilio.
you	your	**Your** house is beautiful.
he	his	**His** book is on the table.
she	her	**Her** family is in Peru.
it	its	**Its** tail is white.
we	our	**Our** car is old.
they	their	**Their** last name is Markov.

Note:

Possessive adjectives replace possessive nouns. Example: _Marco's mother is here_ = _His mother is here._

B Look at the reading "A Family from Mexico." Complete the sentences about Amato with possessive adjectives.

1. Cristo is ____his____ father.

2. Isabel is _____ mother.

3. Amato has a little sister. _____ name is Isabel.

4. Marita and Amato have grandparents. _____ grandparents live with them.

C Complete the sentences. Use the possessive adjectives that relate to each underlined subject pronoun.

1. <u>I</u> am a sociology student. _____*My*_____ name is Yakov.

2. <u>I</u> live with _____ wife and children in a small house.

3. My children are in elementary school. <u>They</u> do _____ homework in the living room.

4. My neighbor has a dog. <u>It</u> eats _____ dinner in the kitchen.

5. My brother's name is Sascha. <u>He</u> lives with _____ wife in California.

6. My sister's name is Sonia. <u>She</u> lives with _____ husband and children in New York.

7. My mother and father live in Russia. <u>They</u> love _____ apartment in Moscow.

8. <u>We</u> visit _____ parents every year.

D Answer the questions. Use possessive adjectives.

1. What is your name? _____ name is _____ .

2. What are your parents' names? _____ names are _____

   and _____ .

3. What room is your class in? _____ class is in room _____ .

4. What is your instructor's name? _____ name is _____ .

5. What color is your instructor's hair? _____ hair is _____ .

6. What is the name of the student next to you? _____ name is

   _____ .

7. What color is the student's eyes? _____ eyes are _____ .

8. What is the title of your class's textbook? The title of _____ textbook is

   _____ .

E **PAIR WORK** Ask a classmate the questions from exercise D.

■ COMMUNICATE

F **WRITE** Write five more questions to ask your partner about students in your class. Use possessive adjectives. Ask your partner the questions.

GRAMMAR AND VOCABULARY Work with four or five students. Sit in a circle. One student shows a partner a picture or drawing of the people in his or her family. This person tells the partner the names and relationships of each person in the picture. Use the grammar and vocabulary from this lesson. Take turns.

This is my uncle. His name is Taku.

The partner shows the picture to the next student in the circle and repeats the information.

 This is Nori's uncle. His name is Taku.

Keep passing the picture around the circle. The last person in the circle gives the picture back to the first person and repeats the information. The first person corrects any mistakes.

This is your uncle. Your uncle's name is Taro.   No! His name is Taku!

PROJECT Make a family information book.

1. Interview three or more members of your family or a family you know.
2. Find out about their likes and dislikes; favorite book, movie, TV show; most important possession; favorite activities; etc.
3. Write a paragraph about each person. You may want to add photos.
4. Present one or more of the paragraphs to your class.

 INTERNET Choose a famous family name (such as Kennedy or Gandhi). Go online. Use that last name and the word "family" as keywords. Learn more about the family. Report back to your class.

VOCABULARY JOURNAL Write sentences for new vocabulary you learned in this lesson.

Example: *My mother's sister is my aunt.*

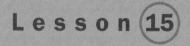

Literature: Shakespeare

■ CONTENT VOCABULARY

Look at the pictures. Do you know the words?

title
characters
author

actor
costume
stage
audience

Write the new words in your vocabulary journal.

■ THINK ABOUT IT

Discuss these questions with a partner.

1. Do you know any plays by Shakespeare? If you do, choose one. What is the title of the play? Who are some of the characters in the play?
2. What is the title of your favorite book? Who is the author? Who are the characters in the book?

■ GRAMMAR IN CONTENT

TR34

A **Read and listen.**

King Lear

Lear is the king of England. He decides to give his kingdom to his three daughters. First he gives **them** a test. He asks **them**: "How much do you love me?" Goneril and Regan are Lear's older daughters. They want his money and power. They tell **him** lies about their love. Lear believes **them**. Cordelia is Lear's youngest daughter. She loves Lear, but she does not talk about her love. This makes Lear angry. He throws **her** out and gives Goneril and Regan his kingdom. The king of France marries Cordelia. He brings **her** to France.

Lear lives first with Goneril and then with Regan. They both treat **him** badly. Lear realizes his mistake. He leaves their houses. He walks around in a storm and slowly loses his mind. Cordelia brings the French army to England to fight for her father. The English army wins the fight. They kill Cordelia and Lear dies from grief.

kingdom: the land and money of a king

power: control

to lose one's mind: to go mad

army: a large group that fights wars

grief: great sadness

Subject Pronouns	Object Pronouns	Examples					
I	me	I	love	him.	He	loves	me.
you	you	You	help	her.	She	helps	you.
he	him	He	calls	you.	You	call	him.
she	her	She	needs	us.	We	need	her.
it	it	It	likes	her.	She	likes	it.
we	us	We	meet	them.	They	meet	us.
they	them	They	write	you.	You	write	them.

Notes:

• Subject pronouns take the place of nouns in the subject position.

  Mary likes John.   =   **She** likes John.

• Object pronouns take the place of nouns in the object position.

  Mary likes **John.**   =   She likes **him.**

B Rewrite the sentences. Replace the underlined words with a subject or object pronoun.

1. My <u>class and I</u> are reading *King Lear*. _____ *We are reading King Lear.*

2. <u>King Lear</u> has three daughters. _____

3. <u>Goneril and Regan</u> are terrible daughters. _____

4. I don't like <u>Goneril and Regan</u>. _____

5. Goneril and Regan tell <u>Lear</u> lies. _____

6. He believes <u>Goneril and Regan</u>. _____

7. <u>Cordelia</u> is a good daughter. _____

8. She really loves <u>Lear.</u> _____

9. He treats <u>Cordelia</u> badly. _____

10. Lear makes <u>me and my class</u> angry. _____

C Complete the sentences with subject and object pronouns.

My name is Ms. Thompson. I'm an English Literature

instructor. __*I*__ teach first year students. I sometimes teach
          (1)

_____ a play by Shakespeare. My students are often confused
  (2)

at first. _____ don't understand the play. They ask _____
         (3)   (4)

many questions. _____ discuss the play together. Then _____
              (5)   (6)

understand _____. Right now _____ are reading *King Lear*.
          (7)   (8)

My students like _____. _____ are writing essays about their favorite character.
                (9)   (10)

Lear is an interesting character. Many students are writing about _____. Some
                                                                   (11)

students are writing about Cordelia. Most students really like _____.
                                                               (12)

■ **C O M M U N I C A T E**

D **WRITE** What is your favorite book? Write the title and the author of the book. Then write a paragraph describing the story. Read your paragraph to the class.

■ GRAMMAR IN CONTENT

A Read and listen.

TR35

Romeo and Juliet

Romeo and Juliet's families are enemies. Romeo meets Juliet at a party. They fall in love. The next day, Friar Lawrence secretly marries them. Juliet's family plans to marry her to another man. The family makes a date for the wedding. Friar Lawrence helps Juliet. **He gives a special drink to her.** The day of her wedding comes. Juliet takes the drink. It puts her to sleep and makes her family think she is dead. Her family puts her in the family tomb. **The Friar sends a message to Romeo.** Romeo doesn't get the message. He thinks Juliet is dead. **A shopkeeper sells poison to Romeo.** He takes it to Juliet's tomb. Romeo drinks the poison and dies. Juliet wakes up. She sees Romeo and kills herself.

enemy: a person that intends harm to another

secretly: a way of doing something without others knowing

tomb: a burial room or grave

poison: a substance that harms or kills

Subject	Verb	Direct Object	*To / For* + Indirect Object
I	give	flowers	to my wife.

Subject	Verb	Indirect Object	Direct Object
I	give	my mother	flowers.

Notes:

• Some sentences have two objects after a verb: a direct object and an indirect object. An indirect object is a person or thing who receives the direct object.

• All sentences with direct and indirect objects can follow the first pattern above (subject + verb + direct object + *to/for* indirect object).

• Sentences with the following verbs can follow both of the patterns above.

To + Direct Object				*For* + Direct Object		
bring	give	tell	show	buy	do	make
e-mail	sell	send	write	cook	get	save

B **Complete each sentence with *was* or *were*.**

1. Wilbur and Orville Wright _____were_____ brothers.

2. Wilbur _____ born in 1867. Orville _____ born in 1871.

3. They _____ the inventors of the airplane.

4. People _____ excited about the first airplane.

5. Mahatma Gandhi _____ the leader of India in the 1920s.

6. Gandhi _____ born in India in 1869.

7. Marilyn Monroe _____ an American movie star in the 1950s.

8. She _____ very beautiful.

9. Many people _____ interested in her.

C **Correct the sentences. There are four mistakes.**

Jackie Robinson were a famous baseball player. He was African American. He is born in 1919. He was the first African American major league baseball player.

The Beatles was a famous rock group. They were British. They are very popular in the 1960s. Ringo Starr was the drummer.

D **Complete each sentence to make a true statement about yourself. Use a time expression (*yesterday, last . . . ,* or *. . . ago*).**

1. I was born _____.

2. I was in primary school _____.

3. I was 12 years old _____.

4. I was at the movies _____.

5. I was with my best friend _____.

6. I was sick _____.

7. I was with my family _____.

8. I was at home _____.

E **GROUP WORK** Look at the sentences your partner wrote for exercise D. Use the sentences to tell your class about your partner.

PART TWO	The Past Tense of *Be*: Negative Statements

■ GRAMMAR IN CONTENT

TR37

A Read and listen.

A Very Famous Woman

This woman was very famous all around the world in the 1990s. Millions of people were interested in her. She **wasn't** a movie star. She **wasn't** an inventor. She **wasn't** an athlete. Who was she?

Answer: Princess Diana

famous: very well-known

million: 1,000,000

interested: wanting to know more

The Past Tense of *Be*: Negative Statements

Subject	*Was / Were* + Not		Contraction		
I	was not	in class yesterday.	I	wasn't	in class yesterday.
He She It	was not	in the U.S. last year.	He She It	wasn't	in the U.S. last year.
You We They	were not	born in the U.S.	You We They	weren't	born in the U.S.

B Look at the reading "A Very Famous Woman." (Circle) the correct answers.

1. Diana ((was not) / were not) an inventor.
2. Diana (was not / were not) a movie star.
3. Diana (was / was not) a princess.
4. Millions of people (were / were not) interested in her.

C These sentences are not true. Rewrite each as a negative sentence. Then use the word(s) in parentheses to write a true sentence.

1. Princess Diana was Spanish. (British)

   _____*Princess Diana wasn't Spanish. She was British.*_____

2. Wilbur and Orville Wright were the inventors of the telephone. (airplane)

   _____

3. Jackie Robinson was born in 1940. (1919)

   _____

4. Pelé was a baseball player. (soccer player)

   _____

5. Marilyn Monroe was a teacher. (movie star)

   _____

6. The Beatles were doctors. (a rock group)

   _____

D Complete each sentence with *was*, *were*, *wasn't*, or *weren't* to make true sentences about yourself.

1. I _____ in Paris last night.
2. My school _____ open yesterday.
3. We _____ in this room yesterday.
4. It _____ cold yesterday.
5. I _____ tired this morning.
6. There _____ students in this class an hour ago.

E WRITE Write four sentences about yourself and your life now. Use the present of *be*. Write four sentences about what was different ten years ago. Use the past of *be*.

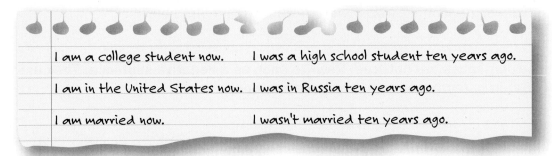

I am a college student now.   I was a high school student ten years ago.

I am in the United States now.   I was in Russia ten years ago.

I am married now.   I wasn't married ten years ago.

Connection Putting It Together

GRAMMAR AND VOCABULARY Choose three famous people or groups of people from the past. Write four sentences about each person or group. Use the grammar and vocabulary from the lesson. Read your sentences to another pair. If they guess the person, they win a point. Take turns.

He was born in 1940.
He was in a famous band.
He wasn't American.

John Lennon?

PROJECT Prepare a report about a famous person.

1. Work with a partner.
2. Choose a famous person from history you want to learn more about.
3. Look for information about the person in the library or on the Internet.
4. Prepare a report about that person.
5. Present your report to the class.

INTERNET Go online. Search for more information about some of the famous people in this lesson. Find out more about these people. Tell your classmates about what you found out.

VOCABULARY JOURNAL Write sentences for new vocabulary you learned in this lesson.

Example: Pelé, Tiger Woods, and Lance Armstrong are <u>athletes</u>.

World History: The Twentieth Century

■ CONTENT VOCABULARY

Look at the pictures. Do you know the words?

explorer

astronaut

scientist

president   first lady

painter

fashion designer

writer

Write the new words in your vocabulary journal.

■ THINK ABOUT IT

Who are the most important kinds of people? Discuss with a partner. Put the people in order of importance. (1 = most important, 12 = least important)

___ inventors	___ rock groups	___ teachers	___ writers
___ movie stars	___ athletes	___ explorers	___ painters
___ presidents	___ scientists	___ astronauts	___ fashion designers

■ GRAMMAR IN CONTENT

A Read and listen.

TR38

History Test

Haru:	I'm studying for my history test. It's about important "firsts" of the twentieth century. I have a couple of questions. You're a history major. Can you help me?
Paco:	Sure.
Haru:	**Were** Edmund Hillary and Tenzing Norgay the first explorers to reach the top of Mount Everest?
Paco:	**Yes, they were.**
Haru:	**Was** Neil Armstrong the first astronaut in space?
Paco:	**No, he wasn't.** He was the first astronaut to walk on the moon. Yuri Gagarin was the first astronaut (or cosmonaut, as they say in Russian) in space.

space: the area beyond Earth's atmosphere

The Past Tense of *Be*: *Yes/No* Questions		
Was/Were	**Subject**	
Was	I	here?
Was	he she it	there?
Were	you we they	first?

The Past Tense of *Be*: Short Answers					
Affirmative			**Negative**		
Yes	**Subject**	**Was/Were**	**No**	**Subject + *Was/Were* + Not**	
Yes,	I	was.	No,	I was not. (I wasn't.)	
	he she it	was.		he was not. (he wasn't.) she was not. (she wasn't.) it was not. (it wasn't.)	
	you we they	were.		you were not. (you weren't.) we were not. (we weren't.) they were not. (they weren't.)	

B Look at the dialogue "History Test." Answer the questions.

1. Were Hillary and Norgay astronauts? _____ *No, they weren't.* _____

2. Were Hillary and Norgay explorers? _____

3. Was Yuri Gagarin the first cosmonaut in space? _____

4. Was Yuri Gagarin the first cosmonaut on the moon? _____

5. Was Neil Armstrong the first astronaut on the moon? _____

C Write *Yes/No* questions. Then write short answers.

1. Nelson Mandela / president of South Africa

   _____ *Was Nelson Mandela the president of South Africa* _____ ? _____ *Yes, he was* _____ .

2. Wilbur and Orville Wright / inventors

   _____? _____.

3. Yuri Gagarin and Neil Armstrong / athletes

   _____? _____.

4. Pablo Picasso / painter

   _____? _____.

5. Tenzing Norgay / writer

   _____? _____.

■ **COMMUNICATE**

D **PAIR WORK** Write a list of *Yes/No* questions to ask your partner about his or her childhood. Then ask your partner the questions. Take turns.

Were you born in the United States?

Were you a good student?

No, I wasn't.

Yes, I was.

GRAMMAR IN CONTENT

TR39

A **Read and listen.**

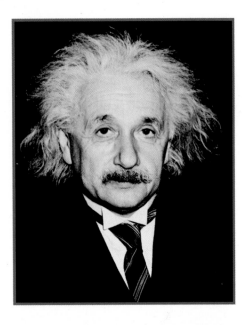

The Person of the Century

Question:	**Who was** *Time* magazine's person of the century?
Answer:	Albert Einstein.
Question:	**When was** he born?
Answer:	1879.
Question:	**Where was** he born?
Answer:	Germany.
Question:	**Why was** Einstein famous?
Answer:	He was a great scientist.

Past Tense *Wh-* Questions with *Be*

Wh- Word	*Was/Were*	Subject		Answer
Who	were	you	with?	My friend. OR I was with my friend.
What	was	Gagarin's	name?	Yuri. OR His name was Yuri.
Where	was	she	born?	India. OR She was born in India.
When	was	she	in Hawaii?	Last year. OR She was in Hawaii last year.
How	was	the weather	yesterday?	Cold. OR It was cold.
Why	were	you	late?	Because I was sick this morning.

Past Tense *Wh-* Questions with *Be* (with *Wh-* Word as Subject)

Wh- Word (Subject)	*Was/Were*	
Who	was	your teacher last year?
Who	were	the Beatles?

Note:

Who can also be used to ask about the subject. Question: *Who was with you?* Answer: *My friend.* OR *My friend was with me.*

B Look at the reading "The Person of the Century." Complete each sentence with a question word and *was* or *were.*

1. ___Who___ ___was___ *Time* magazine's person of the century? Albert Einstein.

2. _____ _____ he famous? He was a great scientist.

3. _____ _____ he born? Germany.

4. _____ _____ he born? 1879.

C Write past tense questions. Then write the answers. Use the information provided.

1. **Question:** Who / Fyodor Dostoevsky ___Who was Fyodor Dostoevsky?___

   Answer: nineteenth-century Russian writer

   ___He was a nineteenth-century Russian writer.___

2. **Q:** Who / the first two U.S. presidents _____

   A: George Washington and John Adams _____

3. **Q:** When / the French Revolution _____

   A: 1789 _____

4. **Q:** Where / Bach and Beethoven born _____

   A: Germany _____

D Put the words in order to make *wh-* questions. Then write answers about yourself when you were a child.

1. you / when / were / born ___When were you born___?

   _____.

2. your / was / who / best friend _____?

   _____.

3. was / what / your favorite subject in school _____?

   _____.

4. your favorite food / what / was _____?

   _____.

5. was / your favorite book / what _____?

   _____.

E PAIR WORK Ask your partner about his or her childhood. Use the questions in exercise D. Add questions of your own. Take notes on your partner's answers. Write a paragraph about your partner's childhood.

Connection | Putting It Together

GRAMMAR AND VOCABULARY With your group, write questions about people, places, and events in history. Use the grammar and vocabulary from the lesson. Each group takes turns asking another group questions. Each group that answers a question correctly gets one point.

Who was president of France in 2000?

Yes, it was. You get one point.

Was it Jacques Chirac?

PROJECT Create a history exam.

1. Work in groups.
2. Create a multiple-choice history exam to give to the other groups.
3. Ask questions about the people in Lessons 16 and 17. Use the Internet or the library to find out more information.
4. Have a class quiz. The group with the most right answers wins!

```
              Our History Exam

1. Nelson Mandela was president of South
Africa between:
a) 1994-1999   b) 1984-1989    c) 1964-1969

2. Pablo Picasso was born in:
a) Russia      b) Spain        c) Slovakia
```

 INTERNET Go online. Find information about famous twentieth-century people. Report back to your class.

VOCABULARY JOURNAL Write sentences for new vocabulary you learned in this lesson.

Example: *Van Gogh and Picasso are famous painters.*

PART 1
The Simple Past Tense of Regular
Verbs: Affirmative and Negative

PART 2
Spelling and Pronunciation of the
Simple Past Tense of Regular
Verbs

PART 3
The Simple Past Tense of
Irregular Verbs

Lesson 18

Business: Successful Business People

■ CONTENT VOCABULARY

Look at the pictures. Do you know the words?

millionaire

Write the new words in your vocabulary journal.

■ THINK ABOUT IT

Work with a group to make a list of the five most important companies in the world today. Do you know who started each company?

■ GRAMMAR IN CONTENT

TR40

A Read and listen.

Levi Strauss

Levi Strauss was born in Germany. He **moved** to the United States in 1829. In 1853 he **opened** a store in San Francisco. Strauss **shared** his business with his nephews and **turned** it **into** a family business. Levi Strauss & Company **manufactured** the first blue jeans. The pants were popular with cowboys and farmers. Today blue jeans are popular with people around the world, and Levi Strauss & Company is still a family business.

manufacture: make

cowboy: a man who works on a cattle ranch

Affirmative Statements		
Subject	**Base Form of Verb + -d/-ed**	
I He She It You We They	**worked**	yesterday.

Negative Statements			
Subject	**Did + Not**	**Base Form of Verb**	
I He She It You We They	**did not** OR **didn't**	**work**	yesterday.

Note: Use the simple past to talk about events that happened and are now finished.

B Look at the reading "Levi Strauss." Is each sentence true or false? Rewrite false sentences correctly.

1. Levi Strauss was born in Italy.   True (False)

   Levi Strauss was not born in Italy. He was born in Germany.

2. He stayed in Germany.   True   False

   _____

3. He moved to the United States in 1829.   True   False

   _____

4. He shared his company with his nephews.   True   False

_____

5. Levi Strauss & Company manufactured the first computers.   True   False

_____

C **Complete the paragraph with the past tense form of the verbs in parentheses.**

> Richard Branson is one of the most successful business people in the world.
>
> He was born in England in 1950. He (start) __*started*__ his first
> (1)
>
> business at the age of 16. It was a magazine for students. He (not graduate)
>
> _____ from high school. He (open) _____
> (2)   (3)
>
> a record store in London. In 1972, he (create) _____ his own
> (4)
>
> record company. He (call) _____ it Virgin Records. The company was very
> (5)
>
> successful. In 1984, he (decide) _____ to start an airline. In 1999, he (add)
> (6)
>
> _____ a cell phone business to his company. Branson now owns more
> (7)
>
> than 200 businesses. Branson also (dream) _____ of adventure. He (want)
> (8)
>
> _____ to fly around the world in a hot air balloon. That (not happen) _____ ,
> (9)   (10)
>
> but in 1987 he (cross)_____ the Atlantic Ocean in a hot air balloon.
> (11)

D **Complete the blanks with the negative past tense form of the verbs in parentheses.**

John wanted to be successful. But instead his manager
fired him. John was a bad employee.

1. He (arrive) __*did not arrive*__ on time for work.

2. He (work) _____ hard.

3. He (listen) _____ to his manager.

4. He (ask) _____ questions.

5. He (fix) _____ problems.

6. He (finish) _____ his work.

E Complete the paragraph with the simple present or the simple past tense of the verbs in parentheses.

The story of Marta's Muffins began a long time ago. Fifteen years ago Marta (work) _worked_ (1) in a bakery. She (want) _____ (2) to be a chef. She (dream) _____ (3) of being successful. Now she (own) _____ (4) the bakery and (have) _____ (5) ten restaurants. Ten years ago, she (dream) _____ (6) of being a millionaire. Now she (dream) _____ (7) of taking a vacation.

■ COMMUNICATE

F **WRITE** Write a paragraph about yourself as a child. Use past tense affirmative and negative sentences.

PART TWO	Spelling and Pronunciation of the Simple Past Tense of Regular Verbs

Spelling of Past Tense of Regular Verbs

Base Form	Past Form	Rule
work walk	worked walked	For most verbs: Add -ed.
live dance	lived danced	For verbs that end in an e: Add -d only.
study cry	studied cried	For verbs that end in a consonant + y: Change y to i and add -ed.
play enjoy	played enjoyed	For verbs that end in a vowel + y: Add -ed.
drop hug	dropped hugged	For one-syllable verbs that end in a consonant + vowel + consonant: Double the final consonant and add -ed.
show relax	showed relaxed	For verbs that end in w or x: Do not double the consonant. Just add -ed.
happen open	happened opened	For two-syllable verbs that end in a consonant + vowel + consonant: If the first syllable is stressed, add -ed. Do not double the consonant.
prefer admit	preferred admitted	For two-syllable verbs that end in a consonant + vowel + consonant: If the second syllable is stressed, double the final consonant and add -ed.

A **Choose the correct spelling of the verbs in this paragraph.**

To: kiya@netmail.net
From: fred@netmail.net
Re: My pay raise!

Hi! How are you? I have a funny story for you. You know I (wantid / (wanted)) a pay raise, right?
                                                                                    (1)
Well, I (typed / typped) an e-mail to my manager. I (asked / askt) him for a raise. He
             (2)   **(3)**
(studyed / studied) my e-mail, and then he (replyed / replied). He (decidded / decided) to
      (4)   **(5)**   **(6)**
give me a raise. I (walkd / walked) to my manager's office and (huged / hugged) him. He
                        (7)   **(8)**
(looked / lookd) shocked. Then he (laught / laughed). It was a good day! Are you having a
       (9)   **(10)**
good day too?

Frederico

B **Write the past tense form of each verb.**

1. like ____liked____   7. use _____

2. stop _____   8. open _____

3. carry _____   9. fix _____

4. cook _____   10. show _____

5. drop _____   11. enjoy _____

6. marry _____   12. listen _____

Pronunciation of Regular Verb Past Tense Forms	
For Verbs That End In . . .	**Pronounce the Ending . . .**
the sounds *p, k, f, s, ch,* or *sh*	/t/ as in "cooked" and "helped"
the sounds *b, g, v, z, zh, th, j, m, n, ng, l, r,* or a vowel sound	/d/ as in "played" and "used"
the sounds *d* or *t*	/əd/ as in "wanted" and "needed"

C Which *-ed* ending do you hear? Put a check (✔) in the correct column.

	/t/ as in "cooked"	/d/ as in "lived"	/əd/ as in "wanted"
1.			
2.			
3.			
4.			
5.			
6.			
7.			
8.			
9.			
10.			

■ **COMMUNICATE**

D **PAIR WORK** Say a verb with a regular past tense form. Your partner will check your pronunciation. Your partner will write the past tense form of the verb. Check your partner's spelling. Take turns.

PART THREE	The Simple Past Tense of Irregular Verbs

■ **GRAMMAR IN CONTENT**

TR42

A Read and listen.

A Success Story

Anita Roddick is the founder of the company called The Body Shop. Roddick **began** with one store. She opened the store in England in 1976. The store **sold** beauty products. She **did not have** business experience, but she **had** good ideas. She **made** natural products. She **put** the products in special containers. People could recycle the containers. She **sold** the products with no advertising. The Body Shop **became** an international success. There are now over 1,980 Body Shop stores in 49 countries. The company has more than 77 million customers.

natural: something made by nature

container: anything used to put or keep things in

recycle: to use again

Affirmative Statements		
Subject	Past Form of Verb	
I He She It You We They	ate	in a restaurant last night.

Negative Statements			
Subject	Did + Not	Base Form of Verb	
I He She It You We They	did not OR didn't	eat	in a restaurant last night.

Notes:

- Irregular verbs do not have the -ed ending in the past tense. Here are some common irregular verbs and their simple past forms.

be / was, were	go / went	meet / met
buy / bought	have / had	pay / paid
come / came	leave / left	put / put
do / did	make / made	see / saw
get / got	sell / sold	take / took
give / gave	speak / spoke	write / wrote

- See the appendix on page 232 for more irregular verbs and their simple past forms.

B Look at the reading "A Success Story." Fill in each blank with the past tense of one of the verbs in the box.

Anita Roddick is the founder of The Body Shop. Roddick
_____began_____ with one store. She _____ the store in England
     (1)   (2)
in 1976. The store _____ beauty products. She _____
                         (3)   (4)
good ideas. The Body Shop _____ an international success.
                                   (5)

become
have
sell
open
~~begin~~

C Complete each sentence with the past tense form of one of the verbs in the box.

Yesterday Jim _____went_____ to the electronics store. He
                      (1)
wanted a cell phone. He _____ with a salesperson about
                               (2)
the different cell phones. The salesperson was very helpful. Jim

_____ a cheap cell phone and _____ it to the counter.
     (3)   (4)
He _____ the cell phone and _____ with a credit card.
        (5)   (6)
The salesperson _____ the cell phone in a bag.
                       (7)

~~go~~
buy
pay
speak
take
put
choose

D Use regular and irregular past tense verbs to complete the sentences about yourself.

1. This morning, I _____.

2. Last night, I _____.

3. Yesterday, I _____.

■ COMMUNICATE

E **GROUP WORK** Write five sentences about your past. Four sentences should be true. One should be false. Use irregular verbs in the simple past tense. Work with a small group. Read your sentences to your group. The group will try to guess the false sentence. Take turns.

Connection | Putting It Together

GRAMMAR AND VOCABULARY Think about the last time you went to a store and bought something. Tell your partner about it. Use the grammar and vocabulary from this lesson.

> Yesterday I went to the mall. I looked in all the clothing stores. I tried on some pants but I didn't like them. The salesperson showed me a nice sweater. I bought it. I paid with a credit card.

PROJECT Write a short biography of an imaginary successful business person.

1. Work with a partner.
2. Make up a story about the life of a successful business person and the business the person started. Answer questions like the following: What is the person's name? When was he/she born? Where was he/she born? What things did he/she do in his/her life? What is the name of his/her business? What does this business do or sell?
3. Work with your partner to write a biography of this person. You may want to use the biographies on pages 134 and 138 as models.
4. Read your biography to the class.

 INTERNET Go online. Find out more about a successful business you know. Take notes on the history of the business. Tell your class what you found out.

VOCABULARY JOURNAL Write sentences for new vocabulary you learned in this lesson.

Example: *I paid for my new computer with a credit card.*

PART 1
The Simple Past Tense: *Yes/No*
Questions and Short Answers

PART 2
The Simple Past Tense: *Wh-*
Questions

Lesson ⑲

Criminology: Crime

■ CONTENT VOCABULARY

Look at the pictures. Do you know these words?

vandalism

murder

theft

police officer

handcuffs

arrest

criminal

jail

fingerprint

Write the new words in your vocabulary journal.

■ THINK ABOUT IT

Discuss these questions with a partner.

1. Did you ever see a crime? If so, what was the crime? Describe what you saw.
2. Make a list of some famous criminals and famous crimes.

■ GRAMMAR IN CONTENT

A Read and listen.

TR43

> ### The Unabomber: An American Criminal
>
> **Student:**   Who is "the Unabomber"?
>
> **Professor:**   He's an American criminal. He sent people bombs in the mail.
>
> **Student:**   **Did** he **kill** anyone?
>
> **Professor:**   **Yes, he did.** He killed three people.
>
> **Student:**   **Did** the FBI **find** him quickly?
>
> **Professor:**   **No, they didn't.** It took 18 years to find him.
>
> **Student:**   **Did** he **have** a trial?
>
> **Professor:**   **Yes, he did.**
>
> **Student:**   Is he in jail now?
>
> **Professor:**   Yes, he is. He's serving a life sentence.

bomb: a weapon that explodes

FBI: the U.S. agency that looks into national crimes

trial: a legal proceeding to decide guilt or innocence

serving a life sentence: in jail for life

The Simple Past Tense: *Yes/No* Questions		Short Answers					
		Affirmative			**Negative**		
Did	**Subject**	***Yes,***	**Subject**	***Did***	***No,***	**Subject**	***Didn't***
Did	I he she it you we they	see the crime?	Yes,	I he she it you we they	did.	No,	I he she it you we they	didn't.

B Look at the dialogue "The Unabomber: An American Criminal." Answer the questions with short answers.

1. Did the Unabomber send bombs in the mail? _____ *Yes, he did.* _____

2. Did he kill anyone? _____

3. Did the FBI find him quickly? _____

4. Did the Unabomber have a trial? _____

C Look at the pictures of the bank robbery. The bank robbery happened an hour ago. Write questions about the robbery. Then write the correct short answers.

1. he have a knife

   Q: _____ *Did he have a knife?* _____   **A:** _____ *No, he didn't.* _____

2. he tie up people

   Q: _____   **A:** _____

3. he hurt anyone

   Q: _____   **A:** _____

4. he have brown hair

   Q: _____   **A:** _____

5. the teller give him money

   Q: _____   **A:** _____

6. the robber put the money in a box

   Q: _____   **A:** _____

7. the teller press the "emergency" button

   Q: _____   **A:** _____

D **PAIR WORK** Student A thinks of a famous crime. Student B asks *yes/no* questions to guess the crime.

Did the crime happen in the United States?

Did the criminal use a gun?

Yes, it did.

No, he didn't.

PART TWO	The Simple Past Tense: *Wh-* Questions

■ G R A M M A R   I N   C O N T E N T

A **Read and listen.**

TR44

> **A Great Museum Theft**
>
> Student: **Where did** the biggest art theft in U.S. history **happen?**
>
> Instructor: At the Isabella Stewart Gardner Museum in Boston.
>
> Student: **When did** it **happen?**
>
> Instructor: On March 8, 1990.
>
> Student: **How did** the thieves **get** the paintings?
>
> Instructor: They dressed in police uniforms and handcuffed the security guards.
>
> Student: **What did** the thieves **take?**
>
> Instructor: Paintings by Vermeer, Rembrandt, and Manet.
>
> Student: **Why did** they **take** the art?
>
> Instructor: Probably because the art was worth $300,000,000.
>
> Student: Did the police catch the thieves?
>
> Instructor: No, they didn't. The frames are still hanging in the museum with no paintings in them.

uniform: a special type of clothing worn by members of a certain group or profession (for example, police officers)

Wh- Questions

Wh- Word	*Did*	Subject	Base Verb	Answers		
What		he	**study?**	Business.	OR	He studied business.
Where		they	**live?**	In Brazil.	OR	They lived in Brazil.
When		she	**leave?**	At 9:00.	OR	She left at 9:00.
Who	did	I	**call?**	John.	OR	You called John.
How		you	**do** on the test?	Very well.	OR	I did very well.
Why		we	**buy** it?	(Because) We liked it.		

Note:

In formal written English, the *wh-* question word for *who* is *whom*. Example: *Whom did the president call?*

Wh- Word as Subject	Past Tense Verb	Answers
Who	called?	Mike. OR Mike called.
What	happened?	It rained.

B Match the questions to the answers.

_b_ 1. Who called?

_____ 2. Why did she call?

_____ 3. Who did they arrest?

_____ 4. Why did they arrest him?

_____ 5. What did he do?

_____ 6. Where did he do it?

_____ 7. Why did he do it?

_____ 8. What did he write?

a. On the wall of the dormitory.

b. Julia called.

c. They arrested Mario.

d. Because he wanted to ask Julia to marry him.

e. She called to tell you the police arrested someone.

f. Because he vandalized school property.

g. "I love you Julia. Marry me."

h. He wrote on a wall.

C PAIR WORK One partner looks at text A. The other looks at text B on page 228. Take turns asking each other past tense *wh-* questions to find the missing information.

Text A: Crimes of the Century

The Great Train Robbery happened in _____ (Where?). The robbery happened on August 8, 1963.

_____ (Who?) robbed the train. They took
(2)
a lot of money. They took _____ (How much?).
(3)
They hurt one person. They hurt the engineer. They hit him

over the head with _____ (What?).
(4)
The police found the robbers' fingerprints. The police caught

_____ (How many?) of the robbers.
(5)

D **PAIR WORK** Ask your partner past tense *wh-* questions about his or her last birthday.

Where did you go?

What did you do there?

I went to a club.

I danced.

Connection | Putting It Together

GRAMMAR AND VOCABULARY Work with a partner. Pretend one person is a police officer. The other is a person who may have committed a crime. Decide on the crime. Then do a role play. Use the grammar and vocabulary from this lesson.

Did you kill Mr. Roberts?

Did you see Mr. Roberts on the night of the crime?

Where did you see him?

No, I didn't.

Yes, I did.

I saw him at a club downtown.

PROJECT **Research a crime.**

1. Work with a partner. Choose a crime you want to learn more about.
2. Look on the Internet to find information about the crime.
3. Learn all you can about the crime. Take notes on what you learn.
4. Tell your classmates which crime or criminal you and your partner learned about.
5. Let your classmates ask you and your partner questions about the crime. Use your notes to try to answer your classmates' questions.

 INTERNET Go online. Search the news headlines on the Internet. Use the keywords "news" and "crime." What crimes happened this week?

VOCABULARY JOURNAL Write sentences for new vocabulary you learned in this lesson.

Example: *People who paint public walls are vandals.*

PART 1
The Past Tense of *Be* and the
Simple Past Tense: Statements

PART 2
The Past Tense of *Be* and the
Simple Past Tense: Questions

Lesson 20

Archaeology: Ancient Egypt

■ CONTENT VOCABULARY

Look at the pictures. Do you know the words?

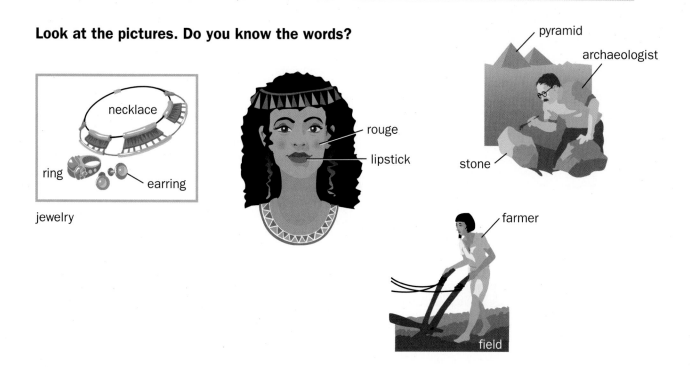

necklace

ring

earring

jewelry

rouge

lipstick

pyramid

archaeologist

stone

farmer

field

Write the new words in your vocabulary journal.

■ THINK ABOUT IT

Discuss these statements with a partner. Do you think each statement is true or false? (You will find the answers in the lesson.)

1. Most ancient Egyptians were farmers.   True   False
2. Ancient Egyptian men and women wore rouge.   True   False
3. The ancient Egyptians believed in life after death.   True   False
4. An archaeologist discovered a pharaoh's tomb   True   False
   in the twentieth century.

■ **CONTENT VOCABULARY**

TR45

A **Read and listen.**

Ancient Egypt

The ancient Egyptians **lived** about 5,000 years ago along the Nile River. Egypt **was** the richest country of the ancient world. Food **was** easy to grow. The Nile **flooded** every year. Farmers **used** the water for their fields.

The pharaohs **were** the rulers of Egypt. The Egyptians **buried** some of their pharaohs in tombs within pyramids. The builders **did not have** modern tools and machines. They **floated** large stones down the Nile River on boats. Then they **carried** the stones and **pushed** them up ramps.

Archaeologists study ancient Egyptian tombs. The paintings and objects inside the tombs help us understand ancient Egyptian culture and life.

pharaoh: a ruler of ancient Egypt

bury: to put a dead person in the ground or a grave

float: to rest or move on top of water

flood: a rising or overflowing of water

The Past Tense of *Be* and Simple Past Tense: Statements		
	Affirmative	**Negative**
The Past Tense of *Be*	She **was** in class yesterday. We **were** at home last night.	She **was not** at home yesterday. We **were not** at school last night.
The Simple Past Tense	He **studied** in the library yesterday. They **lived** in Mexico last year.	He **did not study** at home yesterday. They **did not live** in Argentina last year.

B **Look at the reading "Ancient Egypt." Complete each sentence with the correct past tense form of one of these verbs: *be*, *use*, *bury*, or *live*.**

1. The Egyptians _____lived_____ about 5,000 years ago.

2. Egypt _____ the richest country of the ancient world.

3. Farmers _____ water from the Nile River for their fields.

4. Pharaohs _____ the rulers of Egypt.

5. The Egyptians _____ some of their pharaohs in pyramids.

C Complete the paragraphs. Use the correct past tense form of the verbs in parentheses.

Most ancient Egyptians (be) _____were_____ farmers. They (love) _____
(1)   (2)

good food and drink. They (eat) _____ bread, fish, and vegetables. Beer
(3)

(be) _____ the most popular drink.
(4)

Both men and women (wear) _____ jewelry such as earrings, rings, and
(5)

necklaces. Egyptian women (make) _____ lipstick and rouge from red clay.
(6)

D Read the sentences. Fill in the blanks with the negative form of the underlined words.

1. Most ancient Egyptians <u>had</u> very simple houses. They _____did not have_____ a lot of furniture.

2. Cats <u>were</u> the most popular pets. Birds _____ the most popular pets.

3. The average Egyptian <u>lived</u> to the age of 40. The average Egyptian _____ to the age of 60.

4. Some boys <u>went</u> to school. Girls _____ to school.

5. Divorce <u>was</u> legal. It _____ illegal.

E Correct the composition. There are six more mistakes.

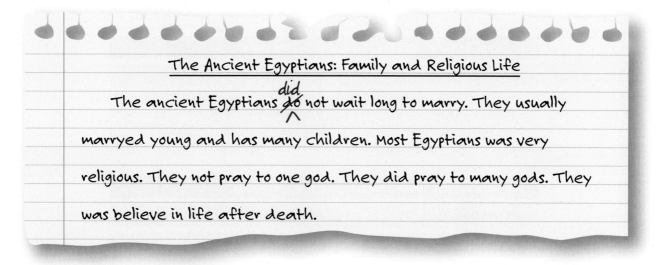

The Ancient Egyptians: Family and Religious Life

                         did

The ancient Egyptians ~~do~~ not wait long to marry. They usually

marryed young and has many children. Most Egyptians was very

religious. They not pray to one god. They did pray to many gods. They

was believe in life after death.

F **WRITE** Write a paragraph about a favorite class you took in the past. Answer questions such as: *What was the class? When did you take it? Was it interesting? Why was it interesting? What did you learn? Did you like the instructor? Why did you like the instructor? Were there many students in the class? Who was in the class?*

PART TWO	The Past Tense of *Be* and the Simple Past Tense: Questions

■ G R A M M A R   I N   C O N T E N T

A Read and listen.

TR46

Tutankhamen's Tomb

Question: **Who was** Tutankhamen?

Answer: He was an Egyptian pharaoh. A British archaeologist named Howard Carter discovered his tomb.

Question: **When did** Carter **discover** the tomb?

Answer: He discovered it on November 4, 1922.

Question: **Did** he **find** many things in the tomb?

Answer: Yes, he did.

Question: **What did** he **find** in the tomb?

Answer: Besides Tutankhamen's body, he found jewelry, furniture, statues, clothes, and other treasures.

discover: find

treasures: valuable things

The Past Tense of *Be*: *Yes/No* and *Wh-* Questions	
Yes/No Questions	*Wh-* Questions
Was she in Egypt? Were you in the museum?	When was she in Egypt? Why were you in the museum?

The Simple Past Tense: *Yes/No* and *Wh-* Questions	
Yes/No Questions	*Wh-* Questions
Did he go on vacation? Did they study archaeology?	Where did he go on vacation? Why did they study archaeology?

Kinds of Noncount Nouns

Type A: Nouns that do not have separate parts. **Examples:** milk, water, cheese, coffee	**Type C:** Nouns that are categories of things. **Examples:** fruit, furniture, money, clothes
Type B: Nouns with too many parts to count. **Examples:** rice, snow, sugar, hair	**Type D:** Nouns that are ideas (you can't touch them). **Examples:** love, crime, information, music

B Look at the reading "Advertising Techniques." Find and (circle) five count nouns. Find and <u>underline</u> five noncount nouns.

C Are the underlined nouns in "Think Before You Spend" count nouns or noncount nouns? Write "C" above the count nouns and "NC" above the noncount nouns.

Think Before You Spend

Advertisers want you to spend your [NC] <u>money</u> on their products. But think before you spend your
(1)

<u>dollars</u>. Ask yourself: Do I really need a new <u>shirt</u>? Do I need another <u>jacket</u>? Or do I already have
(2) **(3)** **(4)**

enough <u>clothes</u>? Should I really eat a <u>hamburger</u> for lunch? Do I really want <u>french fries</u>? Can I find
(5) **(6)** **(7)**

healthier <u>food</u>? Be a smart consumer. And remember—<u>money</u> can't buy <u>happiness</u>.
(8) **(9)** **(10)**

D Some of the sentences have mistakes. Find the mistakes and correct them.

1. I drink ~~coffees~~ *coffee* every morning.

2. She wants a rice.

3. He needs a pen.

4. You have three books.

5. They love a music.

6. Brush your hairs.

■ COMMUNICATE

E PAIR WORK Look through a magazine or newspaper. Make a list of the things you see advertised. Use a dictionary if necessary. Divide the list into two columns. Put all of the count nouns in one column and all of the noncount nouns in the other.

PART TWO	*A/An, Some, Any*

■ GRAMMAR IN CONTENT

TR48

A Read and listen.

Advertising Is Everywhere

Studies show that Americans see about 3,000 ads each day. There are advertisements on television, in newspapers, and on the radio. But they are turning up in **some** new places too. For example, **some** stores now have advertisements on their floors. **Some** public bathrooms now have ads. There are even ads on **some** fruit.

Are there **any** advertisements in space? Not yet, but soon there may be. The Russian space program launched **a** rocket in 2000 with **an** ad for Pizza Hut. There are also **some** companies trying to put ads in space that we can see from Earth.

ads: short form of "advertisements"

turn up: appear

launch: to send up in the air

A/An, Some, and *Any*

	Affirmative Statements	Negative Statements	Questions
Singular Count Nouns	I ate **a** carrot. I ate **an** apple.	I didn't eat **a** carrot. I didn't eat **an** apple.	Do you want **a** carrot? Do you want **an** apple?
Plural Count Nouns	I ate **some** carrots.	I didn't eat **any** carrots.	Do you want **any** carrots? Do you want **some** carrots?
Noncount Nouns	I ate **some** bread.	I didn't eat **any** bread.	Do you want **any** bread? Do you want **some** bread?

Notes:

• *A/an* means "one." Use *a* before a consonant sound. Use *an* before a vowel sound.

• *Some* means "an indefinite amount."

• *Any* is the negative form of *some.* Either *any* or *some* can be used in *yes/no* questions.

B Complete with *a/an* or *some*.

1. _some_ stores   3. _____ money   5. _____ advertisement
2. _____ store   4. _____ dollar   6. _____ advertisements

C Listen and complete the sentences with *a/an*, *some*, or *any*.

TR49

Woman: Look at all of these dirty clothes! I have ___a___ (1) family, _____ (2) job, and _____ (3) busy house. I don't have _____ (4) spare time. I need _____ (5) help! I need _____ (6) answer!

Announcer: This is _____ (1) job for Suds Bright! All you need is _____ (2) washing machine and _____ (3) Suds Bright detergent. You don't need _____ (4) bleach. You don't need _____ (5) stain removers. Suds Bright does it all!

D Complete the sentences and questions with *a/an*, *some*, or *any*. (For some items, either *some* or *any* is correct.)

Daughter: Dad, I need _some_ (1) clothes. Can I have _____ (2) money?

Father: Did your mother give you _____ (3) money for clothes last week?

Daughter: Yes, she did. But I bought _____ (4) jacket. I don't have _____ (5) money left.

Father: Maybe it's time for you to look for _____ (6) job.

Daughter: Um . . . Forget it. I don't need _____ (7) money. I guess I don't really need more clothes.

■ COMMUNICATE

E PAIR WORK What did your partner have for breakfast this morning? Ask *yes/no* questions with *a/an* and *some/any* to find out.

F **PAIR WORK** What items does your partner have at home? Ask "Do you have . . ." questions with *a/an* or *some/any* and the words below. Then ask more questions with words of your own.

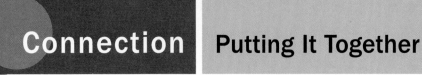

computer	apples	plants
curtains	carpet	air conditioner

Connection | Putting It Together

GRAMMAR AND VOCABULARY Work with a partner. Look through a magazine or newspaper. Your partner will look through a different magazine or newspaper. Take turns telling about the advertisements you see and answering questions about them. Use the grammar and vocabulary from this lesson.

> There are some ads for clothes in my magazine.

> Are there any ads for sneakers?

> Yes. There's an ad for blue and white sneakers. In the ad there's a woman running through a garden. There are flowers and some trees around her.

PROJECT Create an advertisement.

1. Work in groups of three or four.
2. Write an ad for one of the following products: Snaffle Soda, Meow Cat Food, or Luscious Lipstick. Include grammar from this lesson.
3. Show your ad to your class.

 INTERNET Go to your three favorite online stores. Make a list of the things you see advertised. Divide the list into two columns. Put all of the count nouns in one column and all of the noncount nouns in the other.

VOCABULARY JOURNAL Write sentences for new vocabulary you learned in this lesson.

Example: *I am a smart consumer. I buy things I need.*

Business: Tourism

■ CONTENT VOCABULARY

Look at the pictures. Do you know the words?

souvenirs

tourist

GREETINGS FROM SPRINGFIELD

Van Gogh 4/1 - 8/15

museum

beach

park

a postcard

travel agent

traffic

Write the new words in your vocabulary journal.

■ THINK ABOUT IT

Discuss these questions with a partner.

1. What are five popular cities for tourists to visit?
2. What can tourists see and do in these cities?
3. Do tourists like to visit the place where you live? What can they do and see there?

■ GRAMMAR IN CONTENT

TR50

A Read and listen.

Welcome to Malaga

Welcome to Malaga, Spain. I'm the hotel manager here at Hotel Malaga. Malaga is a beautiful city in southern Spain. The weather is wonderful. There is always **a lot of** sunshine. There is **not much** rain. There are **many** things to see and do in our city. For example, there are **many** beaches, **a lot of** restaurants, and **a few** interesting museums.

I want to make sure our guests have the best possible visit. How do I do this? I ask them **some** questions. I learn about their interests. Then I give them **a lot of** advice.

advice: directions or opinions about what to do

Quantity Expressions: Count Nouns (Plural)

Affirmative			Negative		
	Quantity Expression	**Plural Count Noun**		**Quantity Expression**	**Plural Count Noun**
There are	a lot of many **some** a few no	cars.	There aren't There are not	a lot of many any	cars.

Quantity Expressions: Noncount Nouns

Affirmative			Negative		
	Quantity Expression	**Plural Noncount Noun**		**Quantity Expression**	**Plural Noncount Noun**
There is	a lot of some a little no	traffic.	There isn't There is not	a lot of much any	traffic.

Notes:

- Use *many* with count nouns and *a lot of* with count and noncount nouns to talk about a large amount or number.
- Use *a little* with noncount nouns and *a few* with count nouns to talk about a small amount.
- Use *not many* with count nouns and *not much* with noncount nouns to talk about a very small amount or number.

B Complete each sentence with *many* or *much*.

"Hi! I want to travel to Europe. I have __many__ questions.
(1)
I want to visit _____ European countries. I want to see
(2)
_____ museums. I don't have _____ money. I don't have
(3)   (4)
_____ time. I like cities with _____ things to do. But I
(5)   (6)
don't like cities with _____ traffic and noise. I don't have _____ ideas. Do you?"
(7)   (8)

C Complete each sentence with *a few* or *a little*.

"Son, I have __a little__ advice for you. Buy _____
(1)   (2)
bilingual dictionaries. Bring _____ warm sweaters.
(3)
Spend _____ time on the beaches in Portugal. Try
(4)
_____ coffee in Italy. Learn _____ Spanish in
(5)   (6)
Spain. Eat _____ French food in France. Send us _____ postcards.
(7)   (8)
And bring home _____ souvenirs for me."
(9)

D Write true sentences about your city or neighborhood. Use quantity words or phrases.

1. (beaches) _____

2. (history) _____

3. (restaurants) _____

4. (parks) _____

5. (shops) _____

6. (crime) _____

■ **COMMUNICATE**

E **WRITE** Write a paragraph about your city or neighborhood. Use count and noncount nouns and quantity expressions. Use the vocabulary from this lesson.

■ **GRAMMAR IN CONTENT**

A Read and listen.

TR51

Facts about New York City

Question:	**How many** people are there in New York City?
Answer:	There are about 7.5 million people.
Question:	**How many** restaurants are there?
Answer:	There are about 19,500 restaurants.
Question:	**How many** tourists visit each year?
Answer:	About 35 million.
Question:	**How much** money do tourists spend each year?
Answer:	About 15 billion dollars.
Question:	**How much** traffic is there in New York City?
Answer:	There is a lot of traffic.
Question:	**How much** crime is there?
Answer:	There isn't a lot of crime. New York City is one of the safest large cities in America.

How Many/How Much

How Many	Plural Count Noun	
How many	restaurants people	are there in New York?

How Much	Noncount Noun	
How much	traffic crime	is there in New York?

Notes:
* Use *how many* to ask about the quantity of count nouns. Use *how much* to ask about the quantity of noncount nouns.
* Use *how much* to ask about the cost of something. When asking about cost, use *how much* without a noun. Example: *How much ~~money~~ is a train ticket?*

B Complete the questions with *many* or *much.*

1. How ___many___ steps are there in the Statue of Liberty? 354.

2. How _____ windows are there in the Statue of Liberty's crown? 25.

3. How _____ steel is there in the statue? 250,000 pounds.

4. How _____ people visit the statue each year? 4 million.

5. How _____ is a ticket to the Statue of Liberty and Ellis Island? It's free.

6. How _____ traffic is there on Ellis Island? There is no traffic on Ellis Island.

C Complete each question with *how many* or *how much* and one of the phrases in the box.

did you visit	did you see	~~did you meet~~	did you buy
did you hear	did you spend	did you learn	did you write
did you have	did you take		

1. ___How many___ people _____did you meet_____?

2. _____ money _____?

3. _____ music _____?

4. _____ museums _____?

5. _____ art _____?

6. _____ French _____?

7. _____ postcards _____?

8. _____ souvenirs _____?

9. _____ photographs _____?

10. _____ fun _____?

■ **C O M M U N I C A T E**

D **PAIR WORK** Ask your partner about the city or neighborhood he or she grew up in. Ask as many *how many/how much* questions as possible. Your partner should use as many count and noncount nouns and quantity expressions as possible. Take turns.

How many restaurants are there?

There are many restaurants.

GRAMMAR AND VOCABULARY Work with a partner. Tell your partner about your last vacation. Your partner will ask questions to learn more about your vacation. Take turns. Use the grammar and vocabulary from this lesson.

> I was in New York last year. I went to Broadway shows, great restaurants, and interesting museums.

> How many museums are there in New York?

> There are a lot! I went to four or five.

PROJECT Create a tourist brochure for your town or city.

1. Work in pairs.
2. Imagine you work for the tourist information office where you live.
3. Prepare a brochure telling tourists about the places to go and things to see in your town or city. Be sure to use some quantity expressions in your brochure. You may wish to illustrate your brochure with photographs or drawings.
4. Present your brochure to the class.

 INTERNET Is there a country or city you would like to visit? Go online. Search for information about this place. Tell your class what you learned.

VOCABULARY JOURNAL Write sentences for new vocabulary you learned in this lesson.

Example: *I always send my mother a postcard when I travel.*

PART 1
Can: Affirmative and Negative

PART 2
Can: Yes/No Questions and
Short Answers

Lesson ㉓

Health Sciences: Physical Therapy

■ CONTENT VOCABULARY

Look at the pictures. Do you know the words?

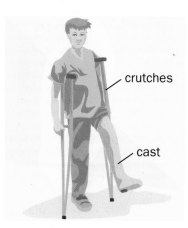

crutches

cast

injury

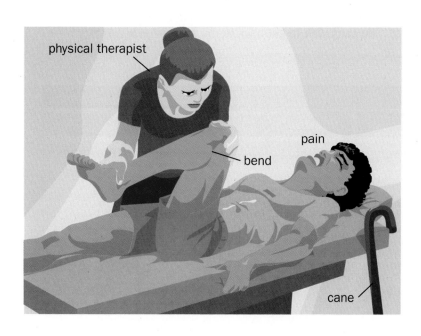

physical therapist

pain

bend

cane

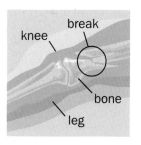

knee

break

bone

leg

Write the new words in your vocabulary journal.

■ THINK ABOUT IT

Discuss these questions with a partner.

1. What are the different ways people can get injured or hurt? Make a list. Use a dictionary if necessary.
2. Have you ever been injured or hurt? How did it happen? How did you get better? Tell your partner about it.

■ GRAMMAR IN CONTENT

TR52

A Read and listen.

A Physical Therapist at Work

I'm Sonia. I'm a physical therapist. The people I work with have injuries or pain. Some of them have broken bones, and some have sports injuries. These problems make it hard for my patients to move parts of their body. I help their bodies move better and become stronger.

Right now I'm working with Keisha. She's a soccer player. She has a knee injury. She **can walk** with a cane now, but she **can't run** and she certainly **can't play** soccer yet. I **can help** her with therapy, exercise, and advice. Her knee is getting better every day. She **can't wait** to get back to the soccer field.

Can: Affirmative and Negative

Affirmative			Negative		
Subject	*Can*	Base Verb	Subject	*Cannot / Can't*	Base Verb
I You He She It We They	can	run.	I You He She It We They	cannot can't	swim.

Notes:
- *Can* expresses ability and possibility.
- The negative form of *can* is *cannot*. The contraction is *can't*.

B Look at the reading "A Physical Therapist at Work." Complete the sentences with *can* or *can't*.

1. Keisha has a knee injury. She ____*can't*____ play soccer now.

2. She _____ walk with a cane.

3. She _____ run.

4. Sonia _____ help Keisha.

5. Keisha _____ wait to play soccer again.

C Listen to the dialogue. (Circle) what Namiko can and can't do.

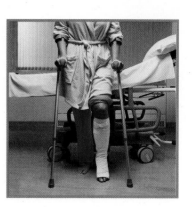

1. She (can / can't) walk without crutches.
2. She (can / can't) drive.
3. She (can / can't) ride her bike.
4. She (can / can't) exercise.
5. She (can / can't) move her leg.
6. She (can / can't) scratch an itch.
7. She (can / can't) relax more now.
8. She (can / can't) do many chores around the house.

D Write a sentence about what each person can or can't do. Use the words and phrases in the box.

| cook | repair a computer | dance | play the violin | drive | cut hair |

1. _____The man can't dance._____

2. _____

3. _____

4. _____

5. _____

6. _____

■ COMMUNICATE

E **GROUP WORK** Make a list of things you can do. Make another list of things you can't do. Tell your group about the things you can and can't do. Your group will discuss your skills and decide on a good job for you.

F **GROUP WORK** Do you have any unusual talents? Can you stand on your head? Can you write with your feet? Tell the class what you can do. If possible, show your group.

PART TWO	*Can*: *Yes/No* Questions and Short Answers

■ GRAMMAR IN CONTENT

TR54

A **Read and listen.**

Mr. Rivera

Physical Therapist:	Mr. Rivera had a stroke a few months ago.
Interviewer:	**Can** he **walk?**
Physical Therapist:	No, he **can't.**
Interviewer:	**Can** he **move** his legs?
Physical Therapist:	Yes, he **can.** He can move them a little.
Interviewer:	**Can** physical therapy **help?**
Physical Therapist:	Yes, it **can.** It can help his legs become stronger.

stroke: a blocked or broken blood vessel in the brain that can cause difficulty moving and speaking and sometimes death

Can: *Yes/No* Questions and Short Answers

Can	Subject	Base Form of Verb		Short Answers	
Can	I you he she it we they	carry	the books?	Yes, I **can.** Yes, you **can.** Yes, he **can.** Yes, she **can.** Yes, it **can.** Yes, we **can.** Yes, they **can.**	No, I **can't.** No, you **can't.** No, he **can't.** No, she **can't.** No, it **can't.** No, we **can't.** No, they **can't.**

Science: In the Laboratory

■ CONTENT VOCABULARY

Look at the pictures. Do you know the words?

laboratory

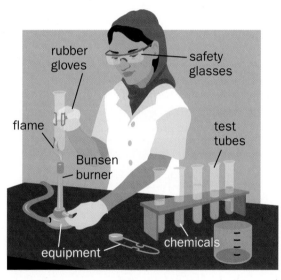

experiment

Write the new words in your vocabulary journal.

■ THINK ABOUT IT

Work with a partner.

1. Pretend to use or put on a piece of laboratory equipment. Your partner will guess the equipment. Take turns.
2. What are important safety rules in a laboratory? Discuss with a partner.

■ GRAMMAR IN CONTENT

TR55

A Read and listen.

LABORATORY SAFETY RULES

1. **Read** the rules carefully.
2. **Wear** rubber gloves and safety glasses at all times.
3. **Wear** shoes or sneakers. **Do not wear** sandals.
4. **Don't eat** or drink in the laboratory.
5. **Keep** your hands away from your face and body during experiments.
6. **Clean** all work areas after experiments.
7. **Turn off** all equipment after experiments.
8. **Wash** your hands after each experiment.

rule: a statement about what must be done   **during:** at the time of

sandals: shoes that do not cover the toes

Imperatives			
Affirmative		**Negative**	
Base Form of Verb		***Don't***	**Base Form of Verb**
Close	the door.	Don't	close	the door.

Notes:

- Use imperatives to:
  a) Give directions or instructions.   Example: *Turn left at the corner.*
  b) Give warnings.   Example: *Be careful!*
  c) Give advice.   Example: *Relax a little.*
  d) Give orders.   Example: *Don't be late!*
  e) Make polite requests (with *please*).   Example: *Please open the window.*
- The subject of imperative statements is always "you," but the subject is not often included in the statement.
- Add "please" to the beginning or the end of an imperative to make a polite request: *Please close the door.* OR *Close the door, please.*

TR56

B Listen to each imperative. (Circle) *Affirmative* or *Negative.*

1. (Affirmative)   Negative   4. Affirmative   Negative
2. Affirmative   Negative   5. Affirmative   Negative
3. Affirmative   Negative   6. Affirmative   Negative

C Match the statements to the correct imperative.

_c_ 1. I need to remember this experiment.   a. Clean it up.

___ 2. I need to look at this slide.   b. Wear rubber gloves.

___ 3. I need a flame.   c. Take notes.

___ 4. I spilled water on the table.   d. Light the Bunsen burner.

___ 5. These chemicals are dangerous.   e. Use a microscope.

D Write a negative imperative for each picture. Use a word or phrase from the box for each sentence.

use your cell phone   eat   ~~drink~~   wear sandals   chew gum   take off your safety glasses

1. _____ Don't drink _____

    in the lab.

2. _____

    in the lab.

3. _____

    in the lab.

4. _____

    in the lab.

5. _____

    in the lab.

6. _____

    during an experiment.

LAB RULES

E Write laboratory safety rules with the words provided. Decide if each should be an affirmative or a negative imperative.

1. come / to the laboratory late _____ Don't come to the laboratory late. _____

2. smoke / in the laboratory _____

3. take / notes on experiments _____

4. smell / the chemicals _____

5. take / laboratory equipment home _____

6. follow / instructions _____

■ COMMUNICATE

F GROUP WORK Imagine a new student is joining your class. Write a list of classroom rules for the student to follow.

G PAIR WORK Work with a partner. Look at the three situations. Brainstorm a list of imperatives to give advice for each situation.

How to Take Care of a Cold	How to Prepare for a Test	How to Prepare for a Job Interview
Get a lot of rest.		

PART TWO | **Polite Requests with *Could You/Would You***

■ GRAMMAR IN CONTENT

TR57

A Read and listen.

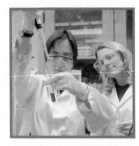

Lab Partners

Lab Partner 1: **Could you** light the Bunsen burner?
Lab Partner 2: Sure.
Lab Partner 1: **Would you** pour the chemicals into the test tubes?
Lab Partner 2: Um . . . OK.
Lab Partner 1: **Could you** heat the chemicals please?
Lab Partner 2: Hey! **Would you** please help me do the experiment?

Polite Requests with *Could You/Would You*

Could/ Would	*You*	Base Form of Verb		Short Answers
Could Would	you	help	me?	Of course. Sure. OK.

Notes:
- Use *could you* and *would you* to ask someone to do something.
- *Please* is often used with *could you* and *would you*. *Please* can come after the subject or at the end of the question. Example: *Could you please close the door?* OR *Could you close the door, please?*

B Look at the reading "Gestures Around the World." Read each sentence and (circle) *True* or *False.*

1. You shouldn't use the American "OK" sign in South America. (True) False
2. You should point with your thumb in the United States. True False
3. You should point with an open hand in Asia. True False
4. You should learn the meanings of gestures in different countries. True False

C Look at the pictures. Then make sentences with the words provided and *should* or *shouldn't.*

1. You ___shouldn't___ yawn in public in Argentina.

2. You _____ show the bottom of your feet in Thailand.

3. You _____ eat with your right hand in Indonesia.

4. You _____ take off your shoes in a home in Saudi Arabia.

5. You _____ shout in Japan.

6. You _____ greet friends with a kiss in Brazil.

D WRITE Imagine a friend is going to your native country. Write a list of things your friend should do and shouldn't do to be polite.

Things You Should Do	Things You Shouldn't Do
You should greet people with a kiss on the cheek.	Don't come to a party without a gift.

E GROUP WORK Make a list of advice for each situation. Use *should* and *shouldn't*. Does your group agree on everything? Are there any cultural differences?

1. Your friend has a job interview tomorrow. What should and shouldn't he or she do at the interview?
2. Your friend is meeting his girlfriend's parents for the first time. What should and shouldn't he do?

PART TWO   *Should*: *Yes/No* Questions and Short Answers

■ GRAMMAR IN CONTENT

TR59

A Read and listen.

Advice for a Business Trip

Jim: I have a business meeting in Japan next month. Could you give me some advice?

Mai: Sure.

Jim: My meeting is with the president of a company. **Should I bow?**

Mai: Yes, you **should**. This shows respect.

Jim: **Should I stand** near him?

Mai: No, you **shouldn't**. It's rude to stand very close to people in Japan.

Jim: **Should I make** eye contact?

Mai: Well, a little eye contact is OK, but you **shouldn't** stare. That's rude.

eye contact: a look directly in the eyes of another person

stare: to look at someone or something steadily

C Fill in the blanks with *must* or *mustn't*.

1. Lawyers _____must_____ be in the courtroom on time.

2. Lawyers _____ listen to the judge.

3. Lawyers _____ argue with the judge.

4. Jurors _____ come to the trial every day.

5. Jurors _____ listen carefully.

6. Jurors _____ talk in the courtroom.

D Look at this poster found outside a courtroom. Then complete each sentence with *must* or *mustn't* and one of the verbs in the box.

use	~~eat~~	be quiet	read	take off

1. You ___mustn't eat___ food in the courtroom.

2. You _____ newspapers in the courtroom.

3. You _____ in the courtroom.

4. You _____ cell phones in the courtroom.

5. You _____ hats and coats before entering the courtroom.

■ COMMUNICATE

E **GROUP WORK** With your group, write two or three sentences about what you must and must not do in each of the following places or situations. Use a dictionary if necessary.

when you are driving   when you are in the library
when you are taking a test   when you are on an airplane

■ GRAMMAR IN CONTENT

TR61

A **Read and listen.**

> ### A Court Reporter
>
> I'm a court reporter. I write down everything people say during a trial. I **have to be** in court every day of the trial. I **have to listen** to the trial very carefully.
>
> Court reporters **have to concentrate**. They also need good grammar and punctuation. I like my job. It's an interesting job, and I **don't have to work** long hours. My sister is a lawyer. She **has to work** all the time.

concentration: total attention to something

Have To/Don't Have To

Subject	Have To/ Has To	Base Verb	Subject	Do Not/ Does Not	Have To	Base Verb
I You We	have to		I You We	do not don't		
They		listen.	They		have to	listen.
He She It	has to		He She It	does not doesn't		

Notes:

- We use *have to* to say that something is necessary. *Have to* is less formal and less urgent than *must*. It is also more common in spoken English. Example: *I need stamps. I have to go to the post office.*

- We use *don't have to* to say that something is not necessary. There is a choice. Example: *I have stamps. I **don't have to** go to the post office.*

B Read each sentence. (Circle) the correct choice.

1. I don't have any money. I ((have to) / don't have to) go to the bank.
2. You can keep this video for three days. You (have to / don't have to) bring it back tomorrow.
3. Please leave your drink outside. You (don't have to / must not) drink in the courtroom.
4. The rent is due on the first day of the month. You (have to / don't have to) pay the rent on time.
5. Today is Wednesday. The museum is free on Wednesdays. You (don't have to / must not) pay today.

C Complete the sentences with *have to, has to, don't have to,* or *doesn't have to* to make true sentences.

1. I _____ speak English in class.

2. My instructor _____ teach at night.

3. I _____ do homework for this class.

4. My instructor _____ teach grammar.

5. I _____ go to school on the weekend.

6. I _____ take a final exam for this class.

D Write sentences using the words provided, *have to* or *don't have to,* and the information in the chart.

Have to . . .	Lawyers	Jurors
be citizens		X
have a law degree	X	
come to court every day of a trial	X	X
speak in court	X	

1. lawyers / citizens _____ Lawyers don't have to be citizens. _____

2. jurors / citizens _____

3. lawyers / have a law degree _____

4. jurors / have a law degree _____

5. lawyers / come to court every day _____

6. jurors / come to court every day _____

7. lawyers / speak in court _____

E What job do you want? Make a list of five things a person with this job has to do and five things the person doesn't have to do. Then compare your list with a partner. How are your jobs similar? How are they different?

I want to be a nurse.

A nurse has to wear a uniform.

I want to be a teacher.

A teacher doesn't have to wear a uniform.

Connection | Putting It Together

GRAMMAR AND VOCABULARY Work with a partner. Each person chooses one of the places below and writes a list of as many rules for behavior in that place as he or she can. Use the grammar and, where appropriate, the vocabulary from this lesson.

a courtroom	an airport	a church, temple, or mosque

Exchange lists with your partner. Do you agree with all the rules on your partner's list? Are there any rules missing? Discuss with your partner.

PROJECT Create a classroom handbook.

1. Work with a group.
2. Brainstorm ideas about proper classroom behavior for students. Discuss what students:
   - must / have to do
   - must not do
   - don't have to do
3. Create a handbook for new students with your group. You may wish to illustrate the handbook.
4. Present your handbook to your class.

INTERNET Look on the Internet for more information about the responsibilities of a juror. Use the keyword phrase "juror handbook." Share what you learned with your classmates.

VOCABULARY JOURNAL Write sentences for new vocabulary you learned in this lesson.

Example: *A juror mustn't speak in court.*

Business: Opening a Restaurant

■ CONTENT VOCABULARY

Look at the pictures. Do you know the words?

hire

check

Write the new words in your vocabulary journal.

■ THINK ABOUT IT

Discuss these questions with a partner.

1. What kinds of people work in a restaurant?
2. What do these people do?

■ GRAMMAR IN CONTENT

TR62

A Read and listen.

Planning a New Restaurant

I'm going to open a Mexican restaurant. It's not going to be like any other restaurant in the neighborhood. The food is going to be delicious. The restaurant is going to be fun and friendly. There is even going to be a mariachi band. My customers are going to love it.

Today I'm going to go to the bank. I need to get a loan for my restaurant. I'm going to show the bank manager my business plan. I have to convince him that my restaurant isn't going to fail. I'm going to prove that it's going to be a big success.

mariachi: a kind of traditional Mexican music

loan: borrowed money that must be paid back with interest

business plan: a description of a business and its goals

convince: to make someone believe something is true

prove: show

Be Going To

Affirmative					Negative				
Subject	**Be**	**Going To**	**Base Verb**		**Subject**	**Be**	**Not**	**Going To**	**Base Verb**
I	am				I	am			
He					He				
She	is				She	is			
It		going to	order.		It		not	going to	drink.
You					You				
We	are				We	are			
They					They				

Notes:

- We use *be going to*:
  1. to talk about the future when plans were made before this moment.

     Example: *I'm going to get married next September.*
  2. to make strong predictions about the future based on current information.

     Example: *I didn't study for the test. I'm going to fail!*
- In informal speech, *going to* is often pronounced as "gonna."

Future Time Expressions

	tomorrow . . .	next . . .	in . . .
tomorrow	. . . morning	. . . week	. . . five minutes
tonight	. . . afternoon	. . . month	. . . an hour
	. . . evening	. . . year	. . . three days
	. . . night	. . . Monday	. . . two weeks

B Look at the pictures. Then complete each sentence with the correct form of *be going to* and a phrase from the box.

clear the table	look at the menus	~~pour water into the glass~~
set the table	pay the check	eat

1. The waiter ___is going to pour___ ___water into the glass.___

4. The woman _____ _____

2. The waiter _____ _____

5. The man and woman _____ _____

3. The men _____ _____

6. The server _____ _____

C Complete each sentence with *am going to* or *am not going to* to make true sentences about yourself.

1. I _____ eat lunch after class.

2. I _____ do homework tonight.

3. I _____ take a test tomorrow.

4. I _____ see my friends this weekend.

5. I _____ be 22 next year.

6. I _____ graduate in two years.

D Complete each sentence with true information about yourself.

Tonight, _____

Tomorrow, _____

Next weekend, _____

Next year, _____

■ COMMUNICATE

E **WRITE** Where are you going to be in ten years? What are you going to be doing? Make predictions about your life, using *going to* and *not going to*.

In Ten Years...

In ten years, I am not going to be in the United States. I'm going to be back in Brazil. I am going to speak perfect English and I am going to start my own English school. I am going to be married to Marta. (Marta is my girlfriend now.) We are going to travel and go to a lot of interesting places. Then we are going to have two or three children.

F **PAIR WORK** Pretend that one of you wants to get together sometime this week. The other person doesn't want to get together and keeps making excuses. Take turns.

Can you meet me on Saturday night?

Can you meet me on Sunday morning?

Sorry. On Saturday night I'm going to the library to study.

No. On Sunday morning I'm going to the gym to exercise.

■ GRAMMAR IN CONTENT

A **Read and listen.**

TR63

Meeting with the Bank Manager

Elisa:	I'm here to talk with you about getting a loan for a restaurant.
Manager:	**Are** you **going to buy** one of the restaurants in town?
Elisa:	No, I**'m not.** I'm going to open a new restaurant.
Manager:	**Where are** you **going to open** the restaurant?
Elisa:	In this neighborhood. I found a nice building on Center Street.
Manager:	**Are** you **going to lease** the building?
Elisa:	Yes, I **am.** I'm very happy with the lease. It's a good price for the location.
Manager:	That sounds good. Alright, Ms. Ramirez, let's look at your business plan . . .

lease: rent for a period of time

location: spot, site

Be Going To: Yes/No Questions

Be	Subject	Going To	Base Verb
Am	I		
	he		
Is	she		
	it	going to	help?
	you		
Are	we		
	they		

Be Going To: Short Answers

Affirmative			Negative	
Yes	Subject	Be	No	Subject + Be + Not
	I	am.		I'm not.
	he			he **isn't.** OR he's **not.**
	she	is.		she **isn't.** OR she's **not.**
Yes,	it		No,	it **isn't.** OR it's **not.**
	you			you **aren't.** OR you're **not.**
	we	are.		we **aren't.** OR we're **not.**
	they			they **aren't.** OR they're **not.**

Be Going To: Wh- Questions

Wh- Word	Be	Subject	Going To	Base Verb
Who	are	you		hire?
What	am	I		do?
Where	is	she		go?
When	is	he	going to	work?
Why	are	we		leave?
How	are	they		pay?

Note:

When "who" or "what" is the subject of an information question, don't use a subject pronoun after *be*. Example: *Who is going to open a restaurant?*

B Look at Elisa's schedule for the week. Write *yes/no going to* questions with the words provided. Then give true answers.

1. She / work on the business plan on Monday

   Q: _Is she going to work on the business plan on Monday_ ? **A:** _Yes, she is_ .

2. She / talk with her accountant on Wednesday

   Q: _____ ? **A:** _____ .

3. She / fill out the loan application on Wednesday

   Q: _____ ? **A:** _____ .

4. She and the bank manager / meet on Thursday

   Q: _____ ? **A:** _____ .

5. She and the chef / discuss the menu on Friday

   Q: _____ ? **A:** _____ .

6. She / buy a computer on Friday

   Q: _____ ? **A:** _____ .

7. She / work on Sunday

   Q: _____ ? **A:** _____ .

C **PAIR WORK** It is now a week before the opening of Elisa's restaurant. One person looks at the Partner A calendar and statements on the following page. The other looks at the Partner B calendar and statements on page 228. Take turns asking each other *wh-* questions with *going to* to find the missing information in your statements.

Partner A Questions

1. On Monday she is going to order _____. (What?)

2. On Wednesday she is going to get _____. (What?)

3. On Friday she is going to pick up the menu from _____. (Where?)

4. On Sunday she is going to _____. (What?)

D Complete the dialogue with *wh- going to* questions.

Ali: I'm excited. I'm going out tonight.

Betsy: Really? _Where are you going to go_ ?

Ali: I'm going to go to a new Mexican restaurant downtown.

Betsy: _____?

Ali: I'm going to go with my family.

Betsy: _____?

Ali: I'm going to order burritos.

Betsy: _____?

Ali: We're going to meet at 8:00.

Betsy: _____?

Ali: We're eating there because we love Mexican food.

■ **COMMUNICATE**

E **PAIR WORK** Ask your partner *yes/no* and *wh-* questions about his or her plans for the future. Use phrases from the box.

| get married | open a business | live in the U.S. | have children | work in an office | travel |

Are you going to get married?

When are you going to get married?

Yes, I am.

When I'm 30.

GRAMMAR AND VOCABULARY Imagine you are going to go out to eat this weekend. Complete the following sentences. Then ask your partner questions to find out about his or her plans. Take turns.

I am going to go to _____. (name of restaurant)

I'm going to go with _____. (name of person)

I'm going to go on _____. (day)

I'm going to go at _____. (time)

I'm going to order _____. (food)

PROJECT Start your own business.

1. Work with a partner. Imagine you will open a business together.
2. Discuss the following questions.

   a. What kind of business are you going to open?
   b. What is your business going to sell?
   c. Where are you going to open your business?
   d. Who are you going to hire?
   e. How are you going to find customers?
   f. How are you going to get the money for the business?

3. Present your idea to the class. Give your classmates a chance to ask you questions about your business.

 INTERNET Go online. Find Web sites for restaurants in your area. Look at the menus. Decide which restaurant you would most like to go to. Plan a visit to the restaurant. When are you going to go? Who are you going to go with? What are you going to order?

VOCABULARY JOURNAL Write sentences for new vocabulary you learned in this lesson.

Example: *We're done with our meal. Can we have the <u>check</u>?*

Medicine: Today and Tomorrow

■ CONTENT VOCABULARY

Look at the pictures. Do you know the words?

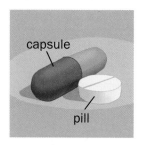

medicine

robot

examination

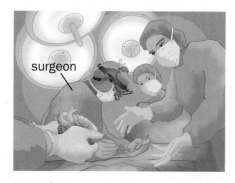

transplant

Write the new words in your vocabulary journal.

■ THINK ABOUT IT

Which of the following do you think are true or possible now? Discuss each statement with a partner.

1. There is a cure for cancer.
2. Robots can do surgery.
3. People can choose the sex of their baby before it is born.

GRAMMAR IN CONTENT

A **Read and listen.**

TR64

"Pills" of the Future

Doctor: I'm writing you a prescription for a new medicine. Take these pills twice every day.

Patient: More pills? Fine. I**'ll take** them twice a day. But I hate swallowing all of these pills.

Doctor: One day there **won't be** any more pills or capsules to swallow.

Patient: What do you mean?

Doctor: One day soon medicine **will come** in tiny computer microchips. Doctors **will put** the microchips under your skin. There **won't be** any pills to worry about.

Patient: That **will be** great!

swallow: to take into the throat through the mouth

tiny: very small

microchip: the part of an electronic device that controls it

skin: the outer covering of a body

Will							
Affirmative			**Negative**				
Subject	*Will*	**Base Verb**	**Subject**	*Will*	*Not*	**Base Verb**	
I You He /She / It We They	will	go.	I You He /She / It We They	will	not	go.	

Notes:

• Use *will*:

  1. to make predictions about the future. Example: *Scientists will find a cure for cancer.*

  2. when the speaker decides to do something at the moment of speaking. Example: *I'm tired. I think I'll go to sleep.*

  3. for promises. Example: *I will be your friend forever.*

• Form the contraction with the subject pronoun and *will*: I will = I'll, You will = You'll.

• The contraction for *will not* is *won't*.

B Listen to each sentence. Decide whether each speaker uses *will* as a prediction, a sudden decision, or a promise.

TR65

	Prediction	Sudden Decision	Promise
1.		X	
2.			
3.			
4.			
5.			

C Complete the sentences with *will* or *won't* to give your opinions about life in the year 2100.

In the year 2100 . . .

1. Most people _____ live to be over 100.

2. Medicine _____ come in computer chips.

3. There _____ be a cure for cancer.

4. People _____ choose the sex of their babies.

5. Robots _____ replace doctors.

6. Brain transplants _____ be possible.

D Correct the mistakes. There are four more mistakes.

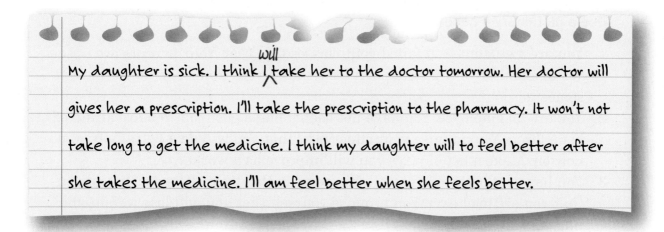

My daughter is sick. I think I ∧ take her to the doctor tomorrow. Her doctor will
will

gives her a prescription. I'll take the prescription to the pharmacy. It won't not

take long to get the medicine. I think my daughter will to feel better after

she takes the medicine. I'll am feel better when she feels better.

E Write a response to each sentence with *will* or *won't* and one of the phrases from the box. Use contractions.

take them when I wake up	go to work today
~~take it to the pharmacy now~~	make an appointment with the receptionist
forget	take them with breakfast

Doctor: Here's your prescription.

Patient: Thanks. _____ *I'll take it to the pharmacy now* _____.

Doctor: Take the pills in the morning.

Patient: Okay. I _____.

Doctor: Take them with some food.

Patient: Okay. I _____.

Doctor: You need to rest today.

Patient: Oh, really? Okay. I _____.

Doctor: I'd like to see you again next week.

Patient: Sure. I _____.

Doctor: Don't forget!

Patient: Don't worry. I _____.

■ COMMUNICATE

F **WRITE** Choose one of the following situations. Write a list of promises with *will*. Use a dictionary if necessary.

1. You are a student. You failed your classes this year. Your parents are upset. Write a list for your parents of all the things you promise to do better next semester.
2. You are an employee. You have not been doing a good job. You are afraid of being fired. You promise your supervisor that you will do a better job from now on. Make a list of ways you will improve as a worker.
3. You have not been feeling well. You went to the doctor. The doctor told you that you are too heavy. You promise yourself that you will lose weight and improve your health. Make a list of ways you will improve your health.

G **WRITE** Write five predictions about the future of medicine. Read the predictions to your class. Do your classmates agree with your predictions?

■ GRAMMAR IN CONTENT

TR66

A **Read and listen.**

Doctors' Exams in the Future

Interviewer: **Will** examinations **be** very different in the future?

Scientist: Yes, they **will.**

Interviewer: **How will** they **be** different?

Scientist: Well, one day doctors will examine patients with a small piece of equipment called a "scanner."

Interviewer: **What will** it **look like?**

Scientist: It will look like a television remote control.

Interviewer: **How will** it **work?**

Scientist: The doctor will hold it over your body and it will find any health problems you have.

Will: Yes / No Questions

Will	Subject	Base Verb
Will	I you he she it we they	go?

Will: Short Answers

Affirmative

Yes	Subject	Will
Yes,	you I he she it we they	will.

Negative

No	Subject	Won't
No,	you I he she it we they	won't.

Will: *Wh-* Questions

Wh- Word	*Will*	Subject	Base Verb
Who		I	visit?
What		you	do?
Where		he	go?
When	will	she	arrive?
Why		we	stay?
How		they	travel?

Note:

When "who" or "what" is the subject of an information question, don't use a subject pronoun after *will*. Example: *Who will pay?*

B Look at the dialogue "Doctors' Exams in the Future." Answer the questions with short answers.

1. Will doctor's visits be different in the future? _____ *Yes, they will.* _____

2. Will doctors examine patients with remote controls? _____

3. Will doctors examine patients with scanners? _____

4. Where will the doctor hold the scanner? _____

5. What will the scanner find? _____

C A drug company is making a new super drug called Fixall. Look at the information about Fixall in the chart. Then write questions and short answers with *will* about the information.

FIX IT ALL WITH FIXALL.

	YES	NO
Help ease headaches	☑	☐
Help ease back pain	☑	☐
Help cure colds	☑	☐
Make you tired	☐	☑
Make you thirsty	☐	☑
Work quickly	☑	☐

1. help headaches _____ *Will it help headaches* _____?
   _____ *Yes, it will* _____.

2. help back pain _____?
   _____.

3. help cure colds _____?
   _____.

4. make you tired _____?
   _____.

5. make you thirsty _____?
   _____.

6. work quickly _____?
   _____.

D Complete the dialogue. Put the words in the right order to form questions and answers.

Scientist: be / robots / will / important in the future of medicine (.)

1. _____Robots will be important in the future of medicine_____.

Interviewer: we see them / will / where (?)

2. _____?

Scientist: will / see them in operating rooms / we (.)

3. _____.

Interviewer: what / they do there / will (?)

4. _____?

Scientist: they / surgery / do / will (.)

5. _____.

Interviewer: will / be / in the operating room too / doctors (?)

6. _____?

Scientist: will / they / yes (.)

7. _____.

Interviewer: the doctors do / will / what (?)

8. _____?

Scientist: they / supervise the robots / will (.)

9. _____.

■ COMMUNICATE

E **PAIR WORK** What do you think the world will be like ten years from now? Ask your partner *yes/no* questions with *will* and the words provided. Then ask more questions of your own. Take turns asking and answering questions.

scientists / find a cure for cancer	people / travel to the moon
brain transplants / be possible	medicine / be in microchips
most people / work from home	a woman / be president of the United States

F Imagine you are a journalist interviewing the president of a drug company. The company will introduce an important new drug next year. You are going to write an article about the drug. Make a list of *wh-* questions with *will* to ask the drug company president.

1. _What will this drug do?_

2. _____

3. _____

4. _____

5. _____

6. _____

7. _____

8. _____

9. _____

10. _____

Connection | Putting It Together

PAIR WORK Work with a partner. Imagine that your partner is from the year 3000. Ask your partner questions about the year 3000. Some topics you might want to ask about are medicine, work, transportation, food, and clothes. Use the grammar and vocabulary from this lesson.

Will food be different in the year 3000?

How will it be different?

Yes, it will.

Food will come in capsules. People will eat a whole meal in one little capsule!

PROJECT Create a new medicine or invention.

1. Work with a group. With your group, decide on the medicine or invention you want to create. Make a list of the things this product will and won't do.

2. Think of a name for your product.

3. Present your product to your class. After your group's presentation, let your classmates ask you questions about your product.

 INTERNET Go online. Look for more information about the future of medicine. Use the keyword phrase "future of medicine." Share what you learned with your class.

VOCABULARY JOURNAL Write sentences for new vocabulary you learned in this lesson.

Example: _My doctor gave me a prescription for new medicine._

PART 1
Comparative Form of Adjectives:
-er and *More*

PART 2
As . . . As/Not As . . . As

Lesson 29

Engineering: Energy Sources

■ CONTENT VOCABULARY

Look at the pictures. Do you know the words?

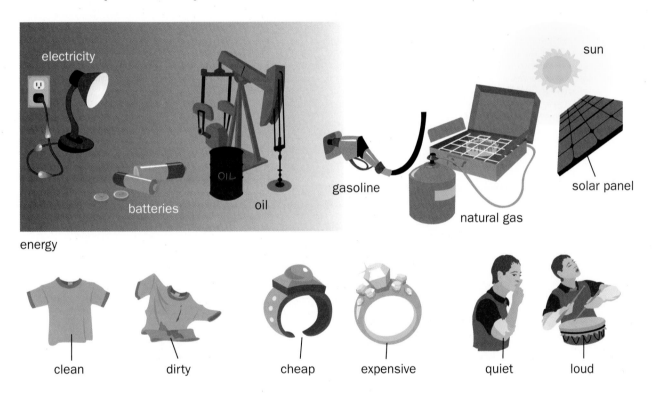

electricity

sun

gasoline

solar panel

batteries

oil

natural gas

energy

clean   dirty   cheap   expensive   quiet   loud

Write the new words in your vocabulary journal.

■ THINK ABOUT IT

Discuss these questions with a partner.

What kind of energy source do you use to:

- heat or cool your home?
- cook your meals?
- listen to music?
- do your laundry?

■ GRAMMAR IN CONTENT

TR67

A Read and listen.

Making Better Automobiles

Automobile engineers are always working on ways to make **better** cars. At the moment, many engineers are working to create electric cars. Why? Traditional cars run on gasoline. The gases cars burn are very bad for the environment. Electricity is much **cleaner than** gasoline. Electric cars are also **quieter**.

So why isn't everybody driving an electric car? Gasoline is a **more efficient** energy source. Cars can run much **longer** on a tank of gasoline **than** on a fully charged battery. To solve this problem, automobile engineers have created hybrid cars. These cars run on both gasoline and electricity. Hybrid cars are still very new, but they are becoming **more popular** each year.

environment: the air, land, and water that people, plants, and things live in

efficient: productive, economical

source: beginning

charge: to load or fill

Comparative Adjectives with *-er*

Subject	*Be*	Comparative Adjective	*Than*	
An electric car	is	cleaner	than	a gasoline car.

Notes:

- For most one-syllable adjectives, add *-er* to form the comparative: *old / older*.
- For one- or two-syllable adjectives that end in *y*, change the *y* to *i* and add *-er: busy / busier*.
- For one-syllable adjectives that end in a single vowel + a single consonant, double the final consonant, then add *-er: big / bigger*.
- Some adjectives have irregular comparative forms.
  Examples: *good / better   bad / worse   far / farther*

Comparative Adjectives with *More*

Subject	*Be*	Comparative Adjective	*Than*	
Electric cars	are	more expensive	than	gasoline cars.

Note:

For adjectives with two syllables or more, place *more* in front of the adjective to form the comparative.

B Complete the sentences with the comparative form of the adjectives in parentheses.

1. Electric cars are (clean) _____*cleaner than*_____ gasoline cars.

2. Electric cars are (quiet) _____ gasoline cars.

3. Gasoline cars are (loud) _____ electric cars.

4. Electric cars are (easy) _____ to take care of _____ gasoline cars.

5. Electric cars are (expensive) _____ gasoline cars.

6. Hybrid cars are (practical) _____ electric cars.

C Write comparative sentences about the cars and people in the picture. Use the words provided.

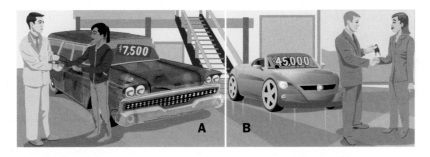

1. car A / car B / old _____*Car A is older than car B.*_____

2. car A / car B / new _____

3. car A / car B / cheap _____

4. car A / car B / expensive _____

5. car A / car B / small _____

6. car A / car B / large _____

7. woman A / woman B / young _____

8. woman A / woman B / old _____

9. woman A / woman B / tall _____

10. woman A / woman B / short _____

■ **C O M M U N I C A T E**

D **PAIR WORK** Take turns creating comparative sentences about each pair of things below. The person who makes the most sentences wins.

| dogs / cats | bicycles / cars | gasoline / electricity | radio / television |

E WRITE Write a paragraph comparing yourself to someone you know well, such as a parent, a brother or sister, or a friend. Share your paragraph with the class.

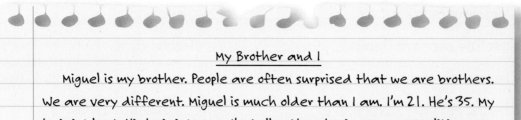

My Brother and I

Miguel is my brother. People are often surprised that we are brothers. We are very different. Miguel is much older than I am. I'm 21. He's 35. My hair is blond. His hair is brown. I'm taller than he is. Our personalities are different too. He's friendlier than I am. I am quieter than he is. But I think I am funnier than Miguel.

PART TWO	*As . . . As/Not As . . . As*

■ GRAMMAR IN CONTENT

TR68

A Read and listen.

A Better Way to Heat Homes

How do you heat your home? You probably use natural gas or oil. I'd like to change that. I'm an electrical engineer. I design solar panels. Solar panels change the sun's energy into heat.

Solar panels are **as effective as** natural gas and oil. But they are **not as common as** natural gas and oil yet, because they aren't **as cheap as** natural gas or oil. But natural gas and oil aren't **as safe as** solar power or **as clean as** solar power. The world needs someone to create a cheaper solar panel. That's my job.

As . . . As/Not As . . . As

Subject	*Be*	*(Not) As*	Adjective	*As*	
My house	is	(not) as	big	as	your house.
Jack's car	is		old		Alex's car.

Notes:

- Use *as . . . as* to say that two people or things are the same in some way.
- Use *not as . . . as* to say that two people or things are not the same in some way.

B Complete each sentence with *as . . . as* or *not as . . . as* and one of the adjectives in the box.

expensive	crowded	dirty	tall	difficult	~~heavy~~

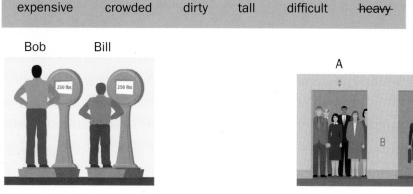

Bob   Bill

1. Bob is _as heavy as_ Bill.

Bob   Bill

2. Bill is _____

_____ Bob.

A   B

A	**B**
2 + 2 = 4	$f(x) = \dfrac{20x}{x^2 + 12}$

3. Equation A is _____

_____ equation B.

4. Elevator B is _____

_____ as elevator A.

5. The ring is _____

_____ the necklace.

6. The pants are _____

_____ the T-shirt.

■ COMMUNICATE

C **PAIR WORK** Talk with your partner and find at least three things that you have in common. Take notes on your conversation. Then tell the class what you have in common, using *as . . . as.*

Marcia and I have a lot in common. She is as tall as I am. Her family is as large as my family. And she is as friendly as I am!

D WRITE Write a paragraph comparing two cities. Use *as . . . as* and *not as . . . as.*

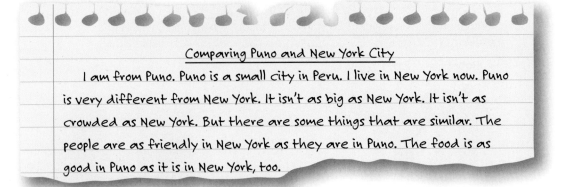

Comparing Puno and New York City

I am from Puno. Puno is a small city in Peru. I live in New York now. Puno is very different from New York. It isn't as big as New York. It isn't as crowded as New York. But there are some things that are similar. The people are as friendly in New York as they are in Puno. The food is as good in Puno as it is in New York, too.

Connection | Putting It Together

GRAMMAR AND VOCABULARY Work with a partner. Find advertisements for two cars in a magazine or newspaper. Look closely at the pictures. Read the advertisements carefully. Discuss and compare the cars. Use the grammar and vocabulary from this lesson.

PROJECT Design a new car.

1. Work with a group.
2. Imagine you are a group of engineers creating a new car. Decide:
   • What energy source will it run on?
   • What will it look like?
   • How fast will it go?
   • How much will it cost?
   • What special features will it have?
3. Present your car to the class. Explain how your car is similar to most cars on the road now. Explain how it is different. Give your classmates a chance to ask questions.

 INTERNET Go online. Look for more information about cars that run both on gas and electricity. Use the keyword phrase "hybrid cars." Share what you learned with your classmates.

VOCABULARY JOURNAL Write sentences for new vocabulary you learned in this lesson.

Example: *I fill my car with gasoline each week.*

PART 1
Past Review: The Simple Past Tense of *Be*, the Simple Past Tense

PART 2
Present Review: The Present Tense of *Be*, the Simple Present Tense, the Present Progressive Tense

PART 3
Be Going To, Will

Lesson (30)

Computer Science: The Past, Present, and Future of Computers

■ CONTENT VOCABULARY

Look at the pictures. Do you know the words?

Personal Digital Assistant (PDA)

download

word processor

MP3 player

online

spreadsheet

database

Write the new words in your vocabulary journal.

■ THINK ABOUT IT

Discuss these questions with a partner.

1. What similar inventions came before the computer?
2. How do people use computers?
3. How will people use computers in the future?

■ GRAMMAR IN CONTENT

TR69

A **Read and listen.**

abacus

ENIAC

Long Before Laptops

It **took** thousands of years for people to create the computer. The first step **happened** about 5,000 years ago. Around this time, the Chinese **invented** the abacus. Before the abacus, people **counted** on their fingers or in their heads. The abacus **was** an important new tool. It **helped** people count much faster.

Thousands of years and many inventions later, an American team **built** the first real computer. The year **was** 1942. The team **called** their computer ENIAC. ENIAC **was** very large. It **was** 8 feet high and 78 feet long and **weighed** 27 tons. But this computer **was** less powerful than one modern home computer.

The Simple Past Tense of *Be*	
Form	**Example**
Affirmative	I **was** in class yesterday.
Negative	He **was not** sick yesterday.
***Yes/No* Questions**	Were you in the computer lab yesterday?
***Wh-* Questions**	Where were the students yesterday?

The Simple Past Tense	
Form	**Example**
Affirmative	I **listened** to my instructor yesterday.
Negative	He **did not feel** well yesterday.
***Yes/No* Questions**	Did you **work** in the computer lab yesterday?
***Wh-* Questions**	Where **did** the students **go** yesterday?

Notes:
- Use the simple past tense of *be* to talk about people, places, and things in the past.
- Use *was* with the subjects *I, he, she,* and *it*.
- Use *were* with the subjects *you, they,* and *we*.
- See Lessons 16, 17, and 20 for more information on the simple past of *be*.

Notes:
- Use the simple past tense to talk about actions that happened in the past.
- Add *-d* or *-ed* to regular past tense verbs in affirmative statements.
- Irregular verbs do not take the *-d/-ed* ending in the past tense. See appendix 4 for irregular verb forms.
- See Lessons 18, 19, and 20 for more information on the simple past tense.

B Look at the reading "Long Before Laptops." (Circle) all the past tense *be* verbs. Underline all the simple past tense verbs.

C (Circle) the correct answers.

The Birth of the Personal Computer

A company called MITS (was created / created) the first home computer. The name of the
                              (1)

computer (was / were) Altair 8000. This computer (was / were) very different from modern computers.
            (2)   **(3)**

People (was not / did not) buy the computer in stores. They (order / ordered) it from the company. It
          (4)   **(5)**

(arrives / arrived) in the mail. It (camed / came) in pieces. People (builded / built) the computer from
   (6)   **(7)**   **(8)**

these pieces. The computer (was not / did not) do many things.
                              (9)

In 1977, Apple (introduces / introduced) a small, useful personal computer. People (buys / bought)
                  (10)   **(11)**

this computer in stores. During the 1980s computers (becomed / became) cheaper. Millions of people
                                                        (12)

(use / used) computers at home. Suddenly, computers (was / were) everywhere.
   (13)   **(14)**

D Read "The Birth of the Personal Computer" in exercise C. Complete each question with *Was, Were,* or *Did.* Then answer each question with a short answer.

1. _____ Microsoft create the personal computer?

2. _____.

3. _____ the Altair 8000 like modern computers?

4. _____.

5. _____ computers popular in the 1980s?

6. _____.

■ **COMMUNICATE**

E **WRITE** Write a paragraph or two about the last time you used a computer.

The Last Time I Used a Computer
I used a computer in the computer lab this morning. It was about 9:30.
There were many other students in the lab. I waited for ten minutes for
a computer. Finally, a woman finished. She stood up and offered me her
computer. I wrote my paper for nursing class on the computer.

■ GRAMMAR IN CONTENT

A Read and listen.

TR70

modern: current, not old-fashioned

chat: to talk online

Computers in Modern Life

Computers **are** smaller, cheaper, and lighter than ever. People **bring** laptops and PDAs everywhere. They **use** word processors, spreadsheets, and databases in places like trains, airplanes, and cafés. The Internet **is** a big part of modern life. People **use** it to chat with friends, pay bills, order groceries, and buy everything from books to cars online. About 75 percent of Americans **use** the Internet, and the average American **spends** about three hours a day online.* Millions of people **are using** the Internet right now!

*Brad Stone, "Hi-Tech's New Day," Newsweek, April 11, 2005, p. 62

The Simple Present Tense of *Be*

Form	Example
Affirmative	I **am** in class.
Negative	He **is not** sick.
Yes/No Questions	**Are** you in the computer lab now?
Wh- Questions	Where **are** the students?

Notes:
- Use *be* to talk about people, places, and things in the present.
- Use *am* with the subject *I*. Use *is* with the subjects *he, she,* or *it*. Use *are* with the subjects *you, we,* and *they*.
- See Lessons 1, 2, and 9 for more information on the simple present tense of *be*.

The Simple Present Tense

Form	Example
Affirmative	I always **listen** to my instructor.
Negative	He **does not feel** well today.
Yes/No Questions	Do you **work** at the computer lab?
Wh- Questions	Where **do** you **go** for lunch?

Notes:
- Use the simple present tense for actions in the present.
- With the subjects *he, she,* and *it* in affirmative statements, add *-s* to most verbs.
- See Lessons 6, 7, 8, 9, and 13 for more information on the simple present tense.

The Present Progressive Tense

Form	Example
Affirmative	I am **listening** to my instructor right now.
Negative	He **was not feeling** well yesterday.
Yes/No Questions	Are you **working** at the computer lab now?
Wh- Questions	Where are the students **going** now?

Notes:
- Use the present progressive tense to talk about actions happening right now.
- To form the present progressive, add *-ing* to most verbs.
- See Lessons 11, 12, and 13 for more information on the present progressive tense.

B Look at the reading "Computers in Modern Life." (Circle) all the present tense of *be* verbs. <u>Underline</u> all the simple present tense verbs. Put a box around all the present progressive verb forms.

C Fill in the blanks with the correct tense and form of the verbs in parentheses.

Carlos: What _are_ you _doing_?

(1. do)

John: I _____ for a computer online.

(2. shop)

Carlos: But you _____ a computer already.

(3. have)

John: I know. But I _____ this computer. It _____ old and slow.

(4. not / like)   (5. be)

Carlos: _____ you _____ a laptop?

(6. want)

John: No. I _____ a PDA.

(7. look for)

Carlos: Why _____ you _____ a PDA?

(8. want)

John: I _____ a computer for home and school. PDAs _____ perfect! They

(9. need)   (10. be)

_____ small and light.

(11. be)

Carlos: _____ they expensive?

(12. be)

John: Yes, they _____.

(13. be)

Carlos: Now what _____ you _____?

(14. do)

John: I _____ onto my bank's Web site.

(15. go)

Carlos: Why?

John: I _____ my balance. Uh-oh.

(16. check)

Carlos: What?

John: I _____ a lot of money in my account. Maybe this old

(17. not / have)

computer _____ so bad after all.

(18. not / be)

D Find and correct the mistakes. (Hint: There are five more mistakes.)

                                    becoming

Personal Digital Assistants are ~~become~~ very popular now. They not have a keyboard

                                                  ∧

or a mouse. Most PDAs doesn't have word processors, spreadsheets, or databases. But

PDAs has a datebook, a clock, a calculator, and a notebook. You can even go on the

Internet with some PDAs. People sends and receives e-mails with these PDAs.

E **PAIR WORK** Tell your partner about a computer, PDA, cell phone, MP3 player, or other electronic device you use. Describe it to your partner. Tell him or her how you use it and what you do with it. Answer any questions your partner has about it. Take turns.

PART THREE	*Be Going To, Will*

■ GRAMMAR IN CONTENT

TR71

A **Read and listen.**

The Future of Computers

Reporter: How **will** our computers **be** different in the future?

Engineer: Computers **are going to get** smaller and smaller. Soon most people **will wear** them. You **will see** the screen on a pair of glasses. You **won't need** a keyboard or a mouse. Computers **will understand** your thoughts and will follow your instructions.

Reporter: **When is** this **going to happen?**

Engineer: It's already beginning to happen!

The Future with *Be Going To*

Form	Example
Affirmative	It **is going to rain** soon.
Negative	She **is not going to graduate** next year.
Yes/No **Questions**	**Are** you **going to use** this computer?
Wh- **Questions**	What **are** you **going to do** tomorrow?

Notes:
• Use *be going to* to talk about plans for the future.
• Make predictions about the future based on current evidence with *be going to*.
• See Lesson 27 for more information about *be going to*.

The Future with *Will*

Form	Example
Affirmative	Computers **will understand** voices in the future.
Negative	I **will not be** late for class.
Yes/No **Questions**	**Will** he buy a PDA?
Wh- **Questions**	What **will** computers **look** like in the future?

Notes:
• Use *will* to make predictions about the future.
• Use *will* when the speaker decides to do something at the moment of speaking.
• Use *will* for promises.
• See Lesson 28 for more information on the future with *will*.

Husband: I _____ see much money in the account.
   (3)

   A) am not   B) don't

Wife: There isn't much money in it right now.

Husband: But we _____ a big check into the account a few weeks ago.
   (4)

   A) is put   B) put

Wife: We _____ that money.
   (5)

   A) spended   B) spent

Husband: What _____ about?
   (6)

   A) do you talk   B) are you talking

Wife: We _____ our rent and our credit card bill last week.
   (7)

   A) did pay   B) paid

Husband: _____ a big credit card bill?
   (8)

   A) Did we have   B) Did we had

Wife: Yes, we _____ the new computer last month.
   (9)

   A) were bought   B) bought

Husband: Oh, that's right.

Wife: Why _____ the computer?
   (10)

   A) are you shut off   B) are you shutting off

Husband: I don't want to look at our bank account anymore!

LEARNER LOG Check (✔) *Yes* or *I Need More Practice.*

Lesson	I Can Use . . .	Yes	I Need More Practice
26	*Must/Must Not* and *Have To/Don't Have To*		
27	Affirmative and Negative Statements and Questions with *Be Going To*		
28	*Will*: Affirmative, Negative Statements and Questions		
29	The Comparative Form of Adjectives: *-Er* and *More, As . . . As,* and *Not As . . . As*		
30	Past, Present, and Future Tense Review		

APPENDIX 1 **Activities for Student B**

LESSON 5, PART 2, EXERCISE F (p. 39)
Student B looks at the picture on this page. Student A looks at the picture on page 39. Find the differences. Ask and answer *is there/are there* questions.

LESSON 5, GRAMMAR AND VOCABULARY (p. 40)
Work with a partner. Partner B looks at the picture on this page. Partner A looks at the picture on page 40. Ask and answer questions to find out how your partner's picture is different from yours. How many differences can you find? Make notes on the differences. Use the grammar and vocabulary from this lesson.

LESSON 11, PART 3, EXERCISE D (p. 91)
Student B looks at the picture on this page. Student A looks at the picture on page 91. Talk about your pictures. Find the differences. Use the present progressive.

LESSON 19, PART 2, EXERCISE C (p. 145)
One partner looks at Text B. The other looks at Text A on page 145. Take turns asking each other past tense *wh-* questions to find the missing information.

Text B: Crimes of the Century

The Great Train Robbery happened in Oxford, England.

The robbery happened on _____ (When?). 15 people
(1)
robbed the train. They took _____ (What?).
(2)
They took 2.6 million pounds. They hurt _____
(3)
(How many people?). They hurt _____ (Who?).
(4)
They hit him over the head with an iron bar. The police found

_____ (What?). The police caught 14 of the robbers.
(5)

LESSON 27, PART 2, EXERCISE C (p. 198)
It is now a week before the opening of Elisa's restaurant. Student B looks at the calendar and statements below. Student A looks at the calendar and statements on page 198. Take turns asking each other *wh-* questions with *going to* to find the missing information in your statements.

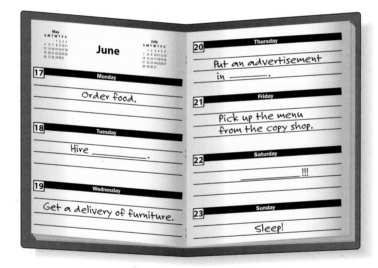

Student B Questions

1. On Tuesday she is going to hire _____.
   (Who?)

2. On Thursday she is going to put an advertisement in _____.
   (Where?)

3. On Saturday she is going to _____.
   (What?)

APPENDIX 2	Glossary

- **Adjective** An adjective describes a noun. Example: *That's a **small** desk.*
- **Adverb** An adverb describes the verb of a sentence or an adjective. Examples: *He is **very** smart. I run **quickly**.*
- **Adverb of Frequency** An adverb of frequency tells how often an action happens. Example: *I **always** go to the library after class.*
- **Affirmative** An affirmative means *yes.*
- **Apostrophe (')** See Appendix 6.
- **Article** An article (*a, an,* and *the*) comes before a noun. Example: *I have **a** book and **an** eraser.*

- **Base Form** The base form of a verb has no tense. It has no ending (-s or -ed). Examples: *be, go, eat, take, write*

- **Capitalization** See Appendix 5.

- **Comma (,)** See Appendix 6.

- **Comparative Form** A comparative form of an adjective or adverb is used to compare two things. Example: *I am **taller** than you.*

- **Consonant** The following letters are consonants: *b, c, d, f, g, h, j, k, l, m, n, p, q, r, s, t, v, w, x, y, z.*

- **Contraction** A contraction is made up of two words put together with an apostrophe. Example: ***She's** my friend.* (She is = she's)

- **Count Noun** Count nouns are nouns that we can count. They have a singular and a plural form. Examples: ***book – books, nurse – nurses***

- **Frequency Expressions** Frequency expressions answer *How often* questions. Examples: ***once a week, three times a week, every day***

- **Imperative** An imperative sentence gives a command or instructions. An imperative sentence usually omits the word *you*. Example: ***Open** the door.*

- **Irregular Verbs** See Appendix 4.

- **Modal** Some examples of modal verbs are ***can, could, should, will, would, must.***

- **Negative** Means *no*.

- **Noncount Noun** A noncount noun is a noun that we don't count. It has no plural form. Examples: ***water, money, rice***

- **Noun** A noun is a word for a person, a place, or a thing. Nouns can be singular (only one) or plural (more than one).

- **Object** The object of the sentence follows the verb. It receives the action of the verb. Example: *Kat wrote a **paragraph.***

- **Object Pronoun** Use object pronouns (*me, you, him, her, it, us, them*) after the verb or preposition. Example: *Kat wore **it.***

- **Period (.)** See Appendix 6.

- **Plural** Plural means more than one. A plural noun usually ends with -s or -es. Examples: *The book**s** are heavy. The bus**es** are not running.*

- **Preposition** A preposition is a short, connecting word. Examples: ***about, above, across, after, around, as, at, away, before, behind, below, by, down, for, from, in, into, like, of, on, out, over, to, under, up, with***

- **Punctuation (. , ' ?)** Punctuation marks are used to make writing clear (for example: periods, commas, apostrophes, question marks). See Appendix 6.

- **Question Mark (?)** See Appendix 6.

- **Regular Verb** A regular verb forms its past tense with -d or -ed. Example: *He **lived** in Mexico.*

- **Sentence** A sentence is a group of words that contains a subject and a verb and expresses a complete thought.

- **Singular** Means one.

- **Subject** The subject of the sentence tells who or what the sentence is about. Example: *The **water** does not taste good.*

- **Subject Pronoun** Use subject pronouns (*I, you, he, she, it, we, they*) in place of a subject noun. Example: ***They*** (= *the books*) *are on the desk.*

- **Tense** A verb has tense. Tense shows when the action of the sentence happened.

    Simple Present: *She occasionally **reads** before bed.*

    Present Progressive: *He **is thinking** about it now.*

    Simple Past: *I **talked** to him yesterday.*

- **Verb** Verbs are words of action or state. Example: *I **go** to work every day. Joe **stays** at home.*

- **Wh- Questions** *Wh*- questions (beginning with *what, when, where, why, who, how*) ask for information. Example: ***Where** is your homework?*

- **Yes/No Questions** *Yes/No* questions ask for a *yes* or *no* answer. Example: *Is she from Mexico? **Yes,** she is.*

APPENDIX 3	Spelling Rules

Spelling of Regular Plural Nouns

Base Form	Plural Form	Rule
book teacher	books teachers	For most plural nouns: Add -*s*
bus box	buses boxes	If the noun ends in *s, z, x, ch, sh:* Add -*es*
dictionary library	dictionaries libraries	If the noun ends in a consonant + *y:* Change *y* to *i* and add -*es*
shelf knife	shelves knives	For some nouns that end in *f* or *fe:* Change the *f* or *fe* to -*ves*
photo tomato	photos tomatoes	If the noun ends with a consonant + *o*, some words take -*s* and others take -*es*.

Simple Present Spelling of Third-Person -*s* Form

Base Form	Spelling with *He, She,* or *It*	Rule
see	sees	Most verbs: Add -*s*
teach	teaches	Verbs that end in *sh, ch, x, z,* or *ss*: Add -*es*
study	studies	Verbs that end in consonant + *y:* Change *y* to *i* and add -*es*

Spelling of Verbs in the -ing Form

Base Form	-ing Form	Rules:
work eat	working eating	For most verbs: Add -ing.
live write	living writing	For verbs that end in a consonant + e: Drop the e and add -ing. Do not double the consonant. Wrong: ~~writting~~
sit plan	sitting planning	For one-syllable verbs that end in one vowel + one consonant: Double the consonant and add -ing.
say sleep listen think	saying sleeping listening thinking	Do not double the last consonant before -ing when the verb: • ends in w, x, or y. • ends in two vowels and then one consonant. • has more than one syllable (when the stress is on the first syllable). • ends in two or more consonants.

Spelling of Past Tense of Regular Verbs

Base Form	Past Form	Rule
work walk	worked walked	For most verbs: Add -ed.
live dance	lived danced	For verbs that end in an e: Add -d only.
study cry	studied cried	For verbs that end in a consonant + y: Change y to i and add -ed.
play enjoy	played enjoyed	For verbs that end in a vowel + y: Add -ed.
drop hug	dropped hugged	For one-syllable verbs that end in a consonant + vowel + consonant: Double the final consonant and add -ed.
show relax	showed relaxed	For verbs that end in w or x: Do not double the consonant. Just add -ed.
happen open	happened opened	For two-syllable verbs that end in a consonant + vowel + consonant: If the first syllable is stressed, add -ed. Do not double the consonant.
prefer admit	preferred admitted	For two-syllable verbs that end in a consonant + vowel + consonant: If the second syllable is stressed, double the final consonant and add -ed.

Common Irregular Past Tense Verbs

Base Form	Simple Past Form	Base Form	Simple Past Form
be	was/were	let	let
become	became	make	made
begin	began	meet	met
break	broke	pay	paid
bring	brought	put	put
build	built	read	read
buy	bought	run	ran
catch	caught	say	said
choose	chose	see	saw
come	came	sell	sold
cost	cost	send	sent
cut	cut	shut	shut
do	did	sing	sang
drink	drank	sit	sat
drive	drove	sleep	slept
eat	ate	speak	spoke
fall	fell	spend	spent
find	found	steal	stole
fly	flew	swim	swam
forget	forgot	take	took
get	got	teach	taught
give	gave	tell	told
go	went	think	thought
have	had	understand	understood
hear	heard	wake	woke
hit	hit	wear	wore
know	knew	win	won
lead	led	write	wrote
leave	left		

Capitalize:

- the first word in a sentence. Example: *The college is closed today.*
- names and titles. Examples: *Manuel, Mrs. Jones, the President*
- geographic names. Examples: *Brazil, Paris, Federal Street, the Atlantic Ocean*
- names of organizations and businesses. Examples: *Boston University, United Nations, Thomson Heinle*
- days of the week, months, and holidays. Examples: *Monday, July, Christmas*
- nationalities, languages, religions, and ethnic groups. Examples: *Russians, English, Islam, Hispanics*
- book and movie titles. Examples: *Grammar Connection, Gone with the Wind*

- Use an **apostrophe (')**:
  1. to show possession. Example: *That is Ivan's pen.*
  2. for contractions. Example: *I didn't (= did not) go to class yesterday.*
- Use a **comma (,)**:
  1. in a list of two or more things. Example: *I have class on Monday, Wednesday, and Friday.*
  2. in answers with *yes* or *no*. Examples: *Yes, I do. No, I don't feel well.*
  3. in statements or questions with *and, but,* or *so*. Examples: *My sister is a student, and she is studying engineering. Kobe is good at math, but Simone is good at art.*
- Use a **period (.)**:
  1. at the end of a sentence. Example: *Francis goes to Hedden Community College.*
  2. after many common abbreviations. Examples: *Mr., Mrs., Dr., Ave.*
- Use a **question mark (?)** at the end of a question. Example: *Do you study math?*

Cardinal Numbers

1	one
2	two
3	three
4	four
5	five
6	six
7	seven
8	eight
9	nine
10	ten
11	eleven
12	twelve
13	thirteen
14	fourteen
15	fifteen
16	sixteen
17	seventeen
18	eighteen
19	nineteen
20	twenty
21	twenty-one
30	thirty
40	forty
50	fifty
60	sixty
70	seventy
80	eighty
90	ninety
100	one hundred
1,000	one thousand
10,000	ten thousand
100,000	one hundred thousand
1,000,000	one million

Ordinal Numbers

first	1st
second	2nd
third	3rd
fourth	4th
fifth	5th
sixth	6th
seventh	7th
eighth	8th
ninth	9th
tenth	10th
eleventh	11th
twelfth	12th
thirteenth	13th
fourteenth	14th
fifteenth	15th
sixteenth	16th
seventeenth	17th
eighteenth	18th
nineteenth	19th
twentieth	20th
twenty-first	21st

Days of the Week

Sunday
Monday
Tuesday
Wednesday
Thursday
Friday
Saturday

Seasons

winter
spring
summer
fall

Months of the Year

January
February
March
April
May
June
July
August
September
October
November
December

Write the Date

April 5, 2004 = 4/5/04

Temperature Chart

Degrees Celsius (°C) and Degrees Fahrenheit (°F)

100°C	212°F
30°C	86°F
25°C	77°F
20°C	68°F
15°C	59°F
10°C	50°F
5°C	41°F
0°C	32°F
−5°C	23°F

Weights and Measures

Weight:

1 pound (lb.) = 453.6 grams (g)
16 ounces (oz.) = 1 pound (lb.)
1 pound (lb.) = .45 kilograms (kg)

Liquid or Volume:

1 cup (c.) = .24 liter (l)
2 cups (c.) = 1 pint (pt.)
2 pints = 1 quart (qt.)
4 quarts = 1 gallon (gal.)
1 gallon (gal.) = 3.78 liters (l)

Length:

1 inch (in. or ")= 2.54 centimeters (cm)
1 foot (ft. or ') = .3048 meters (m)
12 inches (12") = 1 foot (1')
1 yard (yd.) = 3 feet (3') or 0.9144 meters (m)
1 mile (mi.) = 1,609.34 meters (m) or 1.609 kilometers (km)

Time:

60 seconds = 1 minute
60 minutes = 1 hour
24 hours = 1 day
28–31 days = 1 month
12 months = 1 year

Review: Lessons 1–5 (pages 41–42)

A.
1. 's / is
2. 's / is
3. 'm / am
4. 'm / am
5. 'm not / am not
6. 'm / am
7. is
8. isn't / is not

B.
1. c   4. b
2. a   5. d
3. e

C.
1. a
2. students
3. programs
4. libraries
5. students
6. countries
7. a
8. classes

D.
1. This is
2. These are
3. That is
4. This is
5. Those are

E.
1. There are
2. There are
3. There is
4. Is there
5. there is
6. There are
7. There are
8. Is there
9. there is

Review: Lessons 6–10 (pages 83–84)

A.
1. plays   5. do not
2. sings   6. does not
3. knows   7. listen
4. helps   8. helps

B.
1. goes   6. on
2. on   7. has
3. does   8. on
4. on   9. at
5. at

C.
1. What   5. don't
2. Where   6. Do
3. How   7. do
4. Do   8. Who

D.
1. do   5. Do
2. are   6. do
3. Are   7. are
4. are

E.
1. every day
2. twice a week
3. always
4. never
5. How often
6. rarely

Review: Lessons 11–15 (pages 119–120)

A.
1. am watching
2. is reading
3. is showing
4. are not / aren't talking
5. are listening
6. are not / aren't crying
7. are smiling

B.
1. going
2. Is
3. isn't
4. doing
5. No
6. is
7. working

C.
1. writing
2. thinking
3. are
4. cooking
5. is
6. Is
7. reads
8. reading
9. does
10. miss
11. Do

D.
1. João
2. João's
3. His
4. Her
5. Her
6. Their
7. grandparents
8. grandparents'
9. Nina's

E.
1. She
2. They
3. them
4. reads Jane stories /
   reads stories to Jane
5. him
6. him
7. He

8. her
9. They
10. tells a story to Jane /
    tells Jane a story
11. him

Review: Lessons 16–20
(pages 153–154)

A.
1. was   4. was
2. were   5. were not
3. was

B.
1. Where   6. Were
2. Who   7. weren't
3. Was   8. Where
4. was   9. Why
5. wasn't

C.
1. was
2. went
3. wrote
4. did not / didn't graduate
5. dropped
6. started
7. made

D.
1. Did he take
2. Yes, he did
3. What
4. Did the police catch
5. Yes, they did
6. When did they catch

E.
1. was   6. was
2. was   7. Did
3. did   8. had
4. ruled   9. How
5. Was   10. Who

Review: Lessons 21–25
(pages 185–186)

A.
1. any   6. money
2. a   7. dollars
3. any   8. a
4. a   9. a
5. some

B.
1. a little
2. a few
3. many
4. many
5. a little
6. a few
7. How much
8. a few
9. a little

C.
2. Take a seat.
   Would you take a seat,
   please?
3. Open your book.
   Would you open your
   book, please?
4. Work with a partner.
   Would you work with a
   partner, please?
5. Turn off the equipment.
   Would you turn off the
   equipment, please?

D.
1. can
2. Can you
3. can
4. can
5. Can
6. can't

E.
1. Should I
2. Yes,
3. Should I wrap the gift?
4. should wrap

5. Should I shake
6. you should
7. Should
8. No,

Review: Lessons 26–30
(pages 223–225)

A.
1. have to
2. don't have to
3. have to
4. don't have to
5. have to
6. mustn't

B.
1. b   4. c
2. c   5. b
3. b   6. a

C.
1. will
2. 'll
3. won't
4. Will you
5. Will
6. What
7. 'll take
8. I will

D.
1. better
2. more expensive
3. more exciting
4. faster than
5. as fast as
6. prettier
7. more comfortable than
8. not as rich as

E.
1. A   6. B
2. B   7. B
3. B   8. A
4. B   9. B
5. B   10. B

Words in blue are part of the Content Vocabulary section at the start of each Lesson.
Words in black are words glossed with the readings in each lesson.
Words in **bold** are words from the Academic Word List.

Credits

Illustrators

Precision Graphics: pp. 6, 10, 12–13, 15, 18–20, 22, 27 (right), 31–33, 35–36, 38, 43 (left), 51, 57, 66, 69, 78, 88, 99 (top right 3 illustrations), 101, 106, 109, 118, 124, 126, 132, 135, 137, 145, 149, 172, 174–175, 178, 182, 189, 196, 198–199, 206, 212, 213 (only item 3), 214, 215 (top middle illustration and right 3 illustrations), 217, 228

Richard Carbajal/illustrationOnLine.com: pp. 23, 30 (bottom 6 illustrations), 121, 127, 133, 167, 169, 171, 211

Amy Cartwright/illustrationOnLine.com: pp. 155–156, 159–160, 215 (bottom middle illustration), 221

Alan King/illustrationOnLine.com: pp. 161, 163, 165, 213 (all except item 3), 215 (left 2 illustrations)

Katie McCormick/illustrationOnLine.com: pp. 2, 7, 9, 27 (left), 28–29, 43 (right 4 illustrations), 45, 53, 56, 193–195

David Preiss/Munro Campagna.com: pp. 3, 5, 59, 89, 98, 99 (top left), 113, 117, 143, 177

Stacey Previn/Munro Campagna.com: pp. 21, 24, 26, 30 (top), 62, 92, 94–95, 107, 141

Scott Wakefield/Gwen Walters: pp. 4, 39–40, 75, 85, 87, 90–91, 147, 173, 187, 209, 227

Philip Williams/illustrationOnLine.com: pp. 179, 201

Photo Credits

Page 1: Left: © PhotoObjects.net; Left Center: © Alexander Benz/zefa/Corbis; Center: © Bryan Mullennix/Iconica/Getty; Right Center: © PhotoObjects.net; Right: © PhotoObjects.net **Page 2:** Top Left: © PhotoObjects.net; Top Center: © PhotoObjects.net; Top Right: © PhotoObjects.net; Bottom Left: © Royalty-Free/Corbis; Bottom Center: © Charles Gupton/Corbis; Bottom Right: © PhotoObjects.net **Page 8:** © Royalty-Free/Corbis **Page 10:** © Stephen Simpson/Stone/Getty **Page 13:** © Ed Honowitz/The Image Bank/Getty **Page 14:** © Kim Steele/Photodisc Green/Getty/RF **Page 22:** © PhotoObjects.net **Page 33:** © Charles Gupton/Corbis **Page 34:** © Chuck Pefley/Alamy **Page 37:** © Photos.com/RF **Page 44:** © Royalty-Free/Corbis **Page 49:** Top: © Royalty-Free/Corbis; Bottom: © Henrick Sorensen/Photonica/Getty **Page 54:** © Stewart Cohen/Stone/Getty **Page 55:** © Royalty-Free/Corbis **Page 58:** Left: © Karen Moskowitz/Stone+/Getty; Center: © Stockbyte/Getty/RF; Right: © Photos.com **Page 60:** © Getty Images **Page 63:** © Titus Lacoste/Taxi/Getty **Page 64:** © Photos.com **Page 67:** Top Left: © John Giustina/Iconica/Getty; Top Center: © Photos.com; Top Right Center: © Photos.com;

Top Right: © PhotoObjects.net; Bottom Left: © Henry Horenstein/Photonica/Getty; Bottom Center: © PhotoObjects.net; Bottom Right: © PhotoObjects.net **Page 68:** Left: © AFP/Getty Images; Right: © Getty Images **Page 70:** © Anna Clopet/Corbis **Page 76:** © Rob Lewine/Corbis **Page 79:** © Photodisc Green/Getty/RF **Page 86:** © Gaetano Images Inc./Alamy **Page 93:** Top Left: © Royalty-Free/Corbis; Top Right: © Alexander Benz/zefa/Corbis; Bottom: © Photos.com **Page 96:** © Simon Marcus/Corbis **Page 100:** © Shoot/zefa/Corbis **Page 102:** © BananaStock/Alamy/RF **Page 104:** © image100/Alamy/RF **Page 108:** © Bubbles Photolibrary/Alamy **Page 110:** © Stockbyte Platinum/Alamy **Page 114:** © Popperfoto/Alamy **Page 115:** © Thomas Barwick/Photodisc Red/Getty/RF **Page 116:** © Content Mine International/Alamy **Page 122:** Left: © Bettman/Corbis; Left Center: © MinBuZu/Peter Arnold, Inc.; Center: © Bettmann/Corbis; Right Center: © Michael Ochs Archives/Corbis; Right: © Andy Warhol Foundation/Corbis **Page 123:** Left: © Bettmann/Corbis; Right: © Bettmann/Corbis **Page 128:** © 1996 Corbis; Original image courtesy of NASA/Corbis **Page 130:** © Bettman/Corbis **Page 134:** © Doug Norman/Alamy **Page 135:** Top: © Nigel Wright/Pool/Reuters/Corbis; Bottom: © Lawrence Manning/Corbis **Page 138:** © Colin McPherson/Corbis **Page 142:** © Seanna O'Sullivan/Corbis Sygma **Page 144:** © Kevin Flemming/Corbis **Page 145:** © Getty Images **Page 148:** © Jon Arnold Images/Alamy **Page 150:** © John T. Fowler/Alamy **Page 157:** Top Left: © Cephas Picture Library/Alamy; Top Right: © Nikreates/Alamy; Bottom Left: © PhotoObjects.net; Bottom Right: © Photos.com **Page 158:** © Royalty-Free/Corbis **Page 162:** © BananaStock/Alamy/RF **Page 164:** © Photos.com **Page 165:** © Photos.com **Page 168:** © Phototake Inc./Alamy **Page 169:** © Betsie Van der Meer/Stone/Getty **Page 170:** © Photos.com **Page 176:** © Phototake Inc./Alamy **Page 180:** Left: © JG Photography/Alamy/RF; Right: © JG Photography/Alamy/RF **Page 181:** First: © Photos.com; Second: © image100/Alamy/RF; Third: © Pacific Press Service/Alamy; Fourth: © image100/Alamy/RF; Fifth: © Photos.com; Sixth: © PhotoAlto/Alamy/RF **Page 182:** © BananaStock/Alamy/RF **Page 188:** © Comstock Images/Alamy **Page 190:** © Dennis Macdonald/Index Stock Imagery **Page 197:** © Jon Riley/Stone/Getty **Page 202:** © Ryan McVay/Photodisc Green/Getty/RF **Page 205:** © Photodisc Blue/Getty/RF **Page 210:** Top: © Spencer Grant/Photo Researchers, Inc.; Bottom: © Martin Bond/Photo Researchers, Inc. **Page 212:** © Steven Puetzer/Photonica/Getty **Page 216:** Top: © PhotoObjects.net; Bottom: © Jerry Cooke/Corbis **Page 218:** © Tom & Dee Ann McCarthy/Corbis **Page 220:** © Forestier Yves/Corbis Sygma